DISCOVERING TRUE LOVE

A true story of how I learned to love
in very difficult circumstances

H.E. OLSEN

Published by KHARIS PUBLISHING, imprint of
KHARIS MEDIA LLC

Copyright © 2016 H.E. OLSEN

ISBN-13: 978-1-946277-03-9
ISBN-10: 1-946277-03-7

All rights reserved. This book or parts thereof may not be reproduced in any form, stored in a retrieval system, or transmitted in any form by any means - electronic, mechanical, photocopy, recording, or otherwise - without prior written permission of the publisher, except as provided by United States of America copyright law.

All KHARIS PUBLISHING products are available at special quantity discounts for bulk purchase for sales promotions, premiums, fund-raising, and educational needs. For details, write:

Kharis Publishing
709 SW Elmside Drive
Bentonville,
AR 72712
Tel: 1-479-903-8160
sales@kharispublishing.com
www.kharispublishing.com

CONTENTS

	ACKNOWLEDGMENTS	iv
	FOREWORD	v
	PROLOGUE	vii
1	WANTING LOVE STARTS YOUNG	9
2	LIVING BY EMOTIONS	16
3	EMOTIONS OUT OF WHACK	22
4	HITTING BOTTOM	30
5	HEAVENLY INTERVENTION	37
6	BREAKING FREE	41
7	SEEKING TRUTH	44
8	DEATH OF A LOVED ONE	50
9	RUNNING FROM HARDSHIPS	58
10	MEETING MR. RIGHT	66
11	THE BEGINNING OF DARKNESS	73
12	AN ANGEL IN DISGUISE	78
13	SUICIDAL EMOTIONS	81
14	REDISCOVERING LOVE'S TRUE MEANING	88
15	MARRIAGES AND RELATIONSHIPS	94
16	RELATIONSHIPS WITH FAMILY AND FRIENDS	101
17	HAPPILY LOVING AFTER	108
18	DIFFERENT TYPES OF LOVE	110
19	FIGHTING THE GOOD FIGHT	113

ACKNOWLEDGMENTS

I want to thank God for the experiences in my life. These experiences led me to the knowledge of love and what it truly means. I thank the people in my life who have guided me. I want to thank my mom and dad who have taught me that life is what I make it. Also, for giving me a Christian-based background. I want to thank Kathy Croston, Terry West, and Kathleen Fleming, women who became spiritual mothers to me. They have taught me about selflessness, true love, and marriage. I also want to thank Kathy Croston for helping edit part of this book. A big huge thanks needs to go out to my editor. I loved the challenges you gave me. I have learned a great deal. I want to send out a thank you to one of my closest friends, Jacqui Adams (now Jacqui Nelson, congrats); you gave me the experience of a true friendship. We could disagree, fight, and correct each other without losing our bond of friendship. Now, I thank my husband and our three beautiful kids for putting up with me as I wrote this book. Thank you for allowing me to find my path in life. Finally, to my in-laws, even though sometimes it was rough, I believe I wouldn't be on this path without you. The hardships I faced with you brought wisdom and understanding on the subject of love, the greatest gift of all. I send my love to you all!

FOREWORD

It is a delight to write about a young girl that I have known since she was 17 who excels in the area of love. I have watched her go through so many difficult situations with positivity, hope, determination, and sheer will power to do the right thing when everyone around her was not. It is as if she was born to love in the most difficult of circumstances. She has been tested and found to be a true example of 1 Corinthians 13, which is known as the love chapter of the Bible.

Written as a novice writer would write, she brings out the simplest truths about love in a practical way from the setting of her little trailer on a piece of land in the country where other generations of the family dwell. Hardly having any freedom to go about her business as other writers will certainly do, she has captured treasured moments in the middle of the night when she could be alone to write all of these pages about what she has learned about love from her positive and negative experiences, from her "enemy," from God, her in-laws, her parents, her husband, and from her children. I hope that you will treasure what she has captured in the middle of a trial that would have compelled most women to give up and run away. I am sure that you will learn something about love that has escaped you up until now.

Kathleen Croston - Counselor, and Public Speaker

This book is a true story,
but the names of most people and places
have been fictionalized to protect identities of individuals.

PROLOGUE

The past 15 years of my life I have been going through nothing but trials. During those first ten years of struggling, I became buried in hate. Now, I am stronger in love in spite of those trials. In the last five years, I felt healing, I have grown in love, and through this love I have been blessed with a sense of purpose. I want to tell my story. I want to tell the dark secrets and juicy illustrations, even though I am fearful of it. I sit here today finding it easy to write from the passion that comes bubbling out from my struggles and hardships. As I pour my heart out, the cry from my soul, I have found forgiveness for others and forgiveness for myself. As I write my story I often find myself in tears, having to walk away and take breaks. It's amazing that as I open up and zealously write down my sins and hardships they no longer have a hold on me. I am able to let go. With my testimony and the strong desire I have found to write I also found a strong desire to share my story. Writing for myself was one thing but sharing my story is quite another. I have had to fight against the fear of people reading about my life, about my hateful actions. I fought against what I should put down or keep out. After struggling with this for a while I just wrote everything. God knows all my dark secrets and sins. Why do I need to worry about people knowing them?

My story is a quest for love from birth to now. I can look back to the beginning, my earliest memory, and see the road that was set before me. How all my trials and triumphs, hardships and blessings, have brought me to this point in my life. I thought I knew what love was, but I realize now I had absolutely no idea what true love was or is, not until I was surrounded by hate.

The subject of love and what it means has always fascinated me. I have so many thoughts rolling around inside my head. As I continue my journey I am starting to see things in a whole new way. I'm beginning to see that people think they know what love is, but don't have a clue, just like me. That the love we see as truth is nothing but a lie or just a shimmer of what it should be. This brings a feeling of dissatisfaction! I also hear people talk about finding their true love, or, wishing their true love would find them. It's fun to daydream and romanticize about this. I did it all the time. But, it's a moot point. True love isn't dependent on another human being, whose arrival will bring this experience. Love is already there inside of us. Having someone come into our lives, to be the one, is the whipped topping to a desert.

As I study and analyze my past life I'm beginning to see that there can be so much hate surrounding our actions. I also see hateful actions surrounding family relationships and my past friendships. I hope to cover all aspects in this book and share the love that I have found. I also hope that it will bring you to deeply think where you stand on this word love and what it truly means. Remember: this is my opinion based on my beliefs, so don't be afraid to disagree. I also just have to state, for those family members who read this, that this book is written from my point of view. Everyone always has a different version of how things were, are, or seem. This is my version, my feelings, my understanding, and my thoughts on the circumstances around me.

God has given me an amazing testimony to share. He is blessing my path and opening doors. He is guiding my every step. I need to give this my all, and I find that I want to. I want to show the world that we can find love in darkness. I am a living example of it. From my own struggles and imperfect ways, I want to inspire and encourage people to seek and find the truth about love. I want love to shine in your life like it is now shining in mine. If you're up for it, grab a delicious cup of coffee and pretend we're old friends. I hope you enjoy your reading.

H.E. Olsen

1. WANTING LOVE STARTS YOUNG

"For You formed my inward parts;
You covered me in my mother's womb.
I will praise You, for I am fearfully and wonderfully made;
Marvelous are Your works,
And that my soul knows very well.
My frame was not hidden from You,
When I was made in secret,
And skillfully wrought in the lowest parts of the earth.
Your eyes saw my substance, being yet unformed.
And in Your book they all were written,
The days fashioned for me,
When as yet there were none of them."
~Psalm 139:13-16 (NKJV)

I Heather, freckle-faced, brown-haired, and blue-eyed, am a 37 years old woman. For the last several years my husband, three children, and I have lived in a camping trailer with a tip-out on my in-laws' property. Life here has not been easy. Seeking love before and during marriage wasn't easy. In fact, it became a major let down. Every day for the last two years I have been pouring out my heart and soul through writing. I sat at the table in the tip-out staring out the big square window—rain or shine—putting all my feelings, emotions, and thoughts into words. Writing became an outlet that brought healing.

While I wrote, a desire arose in me to share my story by using my mistakes, hardships, and how I overcame my struggles to inspire and encourage others. As I wrote I started to see certain patterns from my past connecting to how I react now, in the present. I saw how my actions back then were affecting me and my relationships. I decided to study up on this. I would become deep in thought as I studied my behavioral dysfunctions from the past seeking answers. I fought through a step-by-step process as I did some deep soul searching and wrote my story. I didn't understand the turn my life had taken in the last decade. But, as I sit here now, I see that God was with me through my entire journey. He fashioned for me days that would bring me to discover true love.

I'm the first child born to Patty and Gary in Silverton, Oregon on March 19, 1979. I've always believed in God. I've always believed that God is a God of love and that He is the rock I'm supposed to stand on, which should make love my center. I thought love was at my center but now I see that I didn't understand the true meaning of love. God made me, us, in His image. So, whether we believe or not we all have love in us, and a desire for love, even if we don't understand it. "And the Lord God formed man of the dust of the ground, and breathed into his nostrils the breath of life; and man became a living being," Genesis 2:7. "So God created man in his own image; in the image of God He created him; male and female He created them," Genesis 1:27. No matter why we were created, or what God's will is for our personal lives, we all are created from His love and are called to love. As I'm sitting here thinking and analyzing the matter, I find that I need to start with my simplest understanding of love. I feel that discovering true love is looking at it from every angle. I want to see where I'm lacking, find the lies that I have believed, and move forward from there.

I don't think we are born to our parents by accident. I believe God places us where he wants us. That with His knowledge of the past, present, and future, He places us where our spiritual needs will have the best potential. Then the evilness of life comes and does its best to take it away, to bring death to the works and will of God. By this, we have an unrealized capacity of who we were meant to be, and a warped way of how we view and understand love among other things.

Sadly, children are born into abusive homes and poverty. Children are also placed in areas of violence. This was not God's will but the will of satan and evil, the will of evil feeding on the hate of people bringing destruction. The parents and past generation who fall into this curse teach children to also be hateful, and the curse continues. If we all chose the will of God, there would be no hateful abuses or violence. We would live with the full capacity of who we are meant to be. We all would be given to kindness, love, and the edification of one another. Good and evil begin to battle for us all while we are in our mothers' wombs. Satan wants to destroy love so we don't know God. "Whoever does not love does not know God, because God is love," 1 John 4:8.

As we are being conceived God breathes life into us, since life is love,

love is what we are created from. This love wants to grow in us. Love or lack of love affects us in some way. Love versus hate starts from the womb. I was told by my midwife during my third pregnancy, "The baby reacts to the emotions of the mother." I've seen the evidence in this with my middle child. Once born, the child feeds off the love or hate from the people who are around. Love is the sunshine that spreads the petals of our soul. It brings life! Without love the child is unhappy, needy, or distant. A negative cloud will hover over this child blocking the sun. The petals of the soul will not flourish, allowing death to take its hold through relational and emotional dysfunctions. Lack of love as a child can lead to relational issues later in life. I grew up in a loving home so why did I have this overwhelming desire to seek love?

We all are made from God's love, whether our parents created us from love or not. Many parents are really good at giving unconditional love to their babies. While we are babies we feel this love, want this love, and grow learning to need this love. It's a part of us. While I was in the womb and from birth I depended on the love of my parents. Being born into a complete family gave me acceptance and love from the beginning. Of course, getting doted on and spoiled by family members doesn't help. I was the first girl grandchild on my dad's side so my grandmother spoiled me rotten, and I'm sure I had lots of attention from my mom's side since she had five sisters and six brothers. Yes, my mom's mom had twelve children. You can just imagine how many relatives I have now, probably in the hundreds. Grandma Whitaker, who wore her curly grey hair short and who I only saw in a muumuu, was a loving and caring woman that always had food for anyone who came through the door.

I loved being a part of this big family, although some of my aunts and uncles were a bit scary to me with their backwoods rugged looks and loud personalities. My mother's side of the family is very outspoken. They tell you what's what from their point of view, not caring what others think. When I was old enough not to be chased away, I would often sit with the grownups at the family reunions, listening to my aunts argue. I would watch their excitement as they forcefully told their different points of view. It's a bit scary how many different points of view there can be. One aunt might like chicken noodle soup plain, while another says it's best with pepper added to it, and then another would chime in, "No, you need to add milk!" It never ended. I really liked it when they started on each other's relationships. I was fascinated by how many different views could be on a relationship. Some of the aunts in this family could be very domineering. I would watch them try to push their will on their brothers and husbands. My uncles were not the kind you could really push around.

No matter how loud the arguments got, it always felt like family. It was home. There was always an uncle, aunt, or cousin to help out when someone else in the family was in need. If someone had a car broke down, a family member would be there to help. If someone was trying to kick a drug addiction, they would find support. If a marriage was falling apart and a home was being lost, the family would chip in. There were always hugs and kisses.

They told me I was a good girl. My large family always expressed "ooh!" and, "aah!" over my artwork and creativity, and then proceeded to tell me how to improve or what they would do differently. I loved my families' imperfections. They created some of my best memories.

I had a strong connection to my Dad at a young age. When I was one or two we were visiting someone in Story Mills, a small, one-store town close to Silverton. This heavy set man wanted to hold me and my dad handed me to him. His eyes, shifty and strange, seemed to contain a strange desire. I can still feel the sensation that something about this man was not right. I can't really say if I didn't like the way this man spoke to me or held me, or if he was too touchy-feely. I lifted my arms to my dad and started to whimper. My dad picked me back up and people laughed. I did not think it was funny and clung to my dad who said, "I'm sorry! She's not normally like this." I'm glad I had a dad who I felt protected and secure with, who responded to my needs even when he couldn't see what I saw, or feel what I felt. I was happy and content, feeling loved by my parents. But my life was about to change. Mom was going to have another baby.

My sister Holly was born in Story Mills on Granny Whitaker's bed. My parents decided to move to Idaho so after Holly's birth they bought six acres of property, sight unseen, from Mother Earth Magazine. I was three, dealing with the huge adjustment of having a baby in the family who stole attention away from me, and moving far away into the woods. I remember being stuffed in my dad's truck looking out the back window, worried that our dog, Cheeko, was going to jump out of the bed of the truck. It happened. My dad called and called but to no avail. We never saw the dog again. This was my first hurt of having something I loved ripped away.

Animals are easy to love because they return affection. Feeling connected to them seems magical. My parents influenced my love for animals and farm life by including me in the farm chores and making them fun. We had our chickens that I would help Mom gather eggs from, and of course our cute playful baby goats that we fed in the cabin with bottles. Horses soon became my favorite animal. Their majestic strength, fairytale-like aura, and gracefulness captivated me. At the age of four I had my first black and white pony named Storm, my favorite of all our animals. I was in animal heaven. Life, for me, was perfect!

My parents were trying to live "Wilderness Family style" in the upper panhandle of Idaho near Cottonwood Creek and close to Friar Lake. The *Wilderness Family* is a movie about a family who leaves civilization for the wilderness to live off the land. We lived in a cabin, just like the characters in the movie, that my dad built using resources from our property to. My parents cut and felled trees, debarked the wood, and cut out grooves so they could stack the lumber like Lincoln logs to erect a 24' x 40' two-story cabin.

A couple of weeks after living in the woods, my Aunt Letta and Uncle James, bought property next to us. I played with my cousins Alex and J.D. as the two cabins were being built. My sister Holly was just a baby who stuck with Mom, not yet play-worthy for the rest of us. Playing with my cousins wasn't always fun and games. One time, when we were at Friar Lake, I was in an inner tube and splashed at Alex. Next thing I knew, he flipped me over into the water. I tried to turn back over but failed. I saw Mom through the hole of the tube run for me. I remember that I felt calm, knowing I should hold my breath until Mom reached me. She pulled me out, checked to see if I was alright, and then lectured Alex. I remember Alex's actions hurting me. Even when there is love in a large family there are acts of hate. But although we sometimes didn't get along, having a close friendship with my boy cousins meant everything to me.

I don't remember much of this time but I do remember that after we moved into the cabin, Mom tried to home school me, but teaching me kindergarten frustrated her to no end. My mom isn't a very patient person. I can still see her turning away and walking off to avoid screaming with frustration. Under her brown bangs her blue eyes were intense. I struggled between the disappointment of letting Mom down and the happiness of not having to do school for a while as I hated school work. It took away from my freedom. I loved playing with the animals, climbing trees, and running around the woods. I was probably a stubborn child. When you're young you don't realize that life must eventually change. If I continued to live this lifestyle I would be a grown wild woman running around the woods of MacAbee falls.

I am blessed to have parents who love unconditionally. Despite my wrong doings and tantrums, they continued to love me. Even when I caused impatience and was being punished I felt loved. My dad would set me down and explain that punishing me hurt him more than it hurt me. He would let me know that he loved me, but because he loved me he wanted me to become a better person. My guilt over hurting my dad was worse than the actual punishment. I didn't like making people angry at me, and I didn't receive punishments often. My parents say that I was an easy child to raise. I'm not sure I believe them.

I never had a close relationship with my sister. One time, I built a huge town out of Lincoln Logs. It took me a long time to build. I had to make sure every piece was perfect. I probably learned this while Dad built the cabin. I left to get my Barbies, and before I returned Holly played Godzilla all through my perfect town. I was angry! I also gave my sister a hard time. I cut bangs in her hair when I was five, and I fought with her over a feather down pillow (the joys of sharing a bed). I believe this is when I started to resent my sister the most. Resentment is a form of hate. It is a negative emotion that doesn't allow us to come close to someone. Although sharing these moments with my sister now brings laughter, it was extremely aggravating as a child.

Being wronged by a sibling can be one of the hardest things to forgive because of family bonds, even in the absence of closeness. The resentment I held for my sister and the resentment she held for me never allowed us to be close. I began to view girls as competition and hard to get along with. It was different with my cousins. I remember sneaking off with my cousins who lived next door. I'm sure I probably disappeared often. They would eat ants while I watched in amazed disgust. We climbed trees and ran all over the woods. We were conquerors of the forest. Our close friendship was based on acceptance of each other. Through them I learned to connect better with boys than with girls.

A year after living at our cabin Mom's sister and her husband, Aunt Paula and Uncle Mick, moved to join us in the area. I remember being at her house playing with my older cousin Shad. We had this great idea to fill the gas tank in Uncle Mick's truck with rocks. We did this for a long time. I'm pretty sure it was almost filled to the top when Uncle Mick barked at us. We ran and hid in the camp trailer, huddling together in a cupboard. Aunt Paula found us with a look of great relief. I don't remember how long we were locked in the cupboard, but it was long enough to make Aunt Paula panic and nearly call a search party for fear that we had drowned in the nearby creek. Shad and I didn't get into much trouble, just a lecture, tempered by the relief of us being found. An hour later we were playing outside again with his older sister, my cousin Haylie who was probably sent out to keep an eye on us. I loved playing with Haylie. I also loved her long blond hair. She was always fun and thought of games for us. I looked up to her. She was the cousin that I always looked forward to seeing. She did steal my baby Strawberry Shortcake doll one Christmas and didn't want to give it back but I still loved her. She was the first girl I really connected to, largely because she was also a tomboy. She would climb trees and play in the mud too.

Dad made childhood fun. He hooked up the little black and white television to the car battery so we could watch Saturday morning cartoons. I loved He-man, my first animated crush. Dad laughed when my friends and I would run around the fenced area like horses, lick the salt rock, and even eat the grain mixed with molasses. Dad built this swing that was really long. I could go so high that I felt that I could touch the sky. One time, I begged my dad to let me ride my Storm down the road by myself. He said I could go to the end of the road and back. I felt so grown-up, but I only got about half way. Storm was acting up, looking off to one side. I felt a tingling go up my spine, so I turned Storm around and went back home. It could have been my imagination, but the feeling was strong. I do believe we have guardian angels who look out for us, but it's up to us to listen. God loves us. He will offer us help through Angels and the Holy Spirit. I told Dad about it after I rode back to the barn. I can still see those understanding, concerned, yet laughing eyes. He said, "Well, I'm glad you came back then!" In my childhood eyes my dad was amazing. As a grownup, I appreciate the goodness in my parents. This also gives me hope that my and my husband's children will also one day see our goodness. The kids will look beyond the mistakes we've made as parents and remember and appreciate the love we gave.

Mom decided she didn't want to home school me the following year so she stuck me in first grade at Friar River Elementary. I was shy, distant, and scared. I rode to the bus stop in my aunt and uncle's rusty little Volkswagen bug with a big hole in the passenger side floor. I would watch the road through that hole while they drove us to the bus stop, always worried I was going to fall through it. On the way home, Alex, J.D., and I would walk the three miles from the bus stop. At first I remember being afraid, but afterwards it became fun. We would play the entire way home. The fears that I struggled with are simple to understand. My world was changing and I was experiencing new things, whether I was ready or not.

I cherish the memory of my brother's birth. We drove two hours into Sandpoint, Idaho for the midwife. I watched my mom go through the process of getting her blood pressure checked. I was even allowed to listen to the baby's heartbeat. I felt connected and a part of this pregnancy. When it came time to have the baby we stayed at a friend's house in Friar River since our place was way out in the boondocks. My sister and I were allowed to watch the baby be born. Mom did a lot of breathing, struggling on the plastic covered mattress. I remember watching in horrified amazement as my baby brother slid out. I loved him instantly. On July 7, 1986, Gary "Levi" joined our crazily large family.

Our world wasn't perfect, but we had each other, even during our less-than-loving actions. My parents never put conditions on their love for us, even when they were angry. They allowed us to be who we were. I learned from them how to love without expecting anything in return. Love in its simplicity with acceptance, connection, and the give-and-take is actually very beautiful. But this didn't stop me from wanting to find love, feeling the need to find a special love, to have a special closeness to someone. It was almost like experiencing love caused me to want more of it. I found by my need to seek love, I made it complicated. I didn't understand. I was learning to be led by my emotions, struggling to be accepted, wanting to be loved by my friends and family.

2. LIVING BY EMOTIONS

*"You ran well. Who hindered you from obeying the truth?
This persuasion does not come from Him who calls you.
A little leaven leavens the whole lump."
~Galatians 5:7-9* (NKJV)

Right now, I'm going through menopause. I started a few months ago. Experiencing the heat flashes, light to heavy menstrual flow, and my wacked out emotions—I'm thankful for the understanding of why I'm reacting the way I am. Today while I'm trying to get some household chores done I feel like closing myself off from the rest of the world and just sleeping. I'm going through some type of weird depression-like symptom for no apparent reason. I'm driving my hubby crazy! My energy and emotions feel zapped. As an adult, I have more control over my emotions and can tell my emotions "knock it off!" When I was a child I couldn't do this. My emotions ruled me. My emotions were controlled by the influences around me. I started thinking of the influences in my first years of school and how those influences shaped me. In grade school, I learned to let my emotions guide my actions. If it felt good, then it was all right. Mix this philosophy with Sunday school and you have a confused girl. I did what felt right even if it contradicted what I learned from the word of God in Sunday school. In my own mind, I believed what felt good was right. I copied my young friends regardless of what they were doing. Then guilt entered my life. Guilt hit hard, turning into conviction, pushing me to do the right thing and not what felt good. I recall a few episodes where I hurt someone's feelings and then felt sorry. This would cause me to take a mental note not to repeat this offence. This all started in Eldertown, Idaho.

My parents sold the cabin and we moved into Eldertown, a community just five miles away from Friar River, right on the Washington and Idaho border. If you're not from here you wouldn't know that Eldertown even existed because it's connected to Newdock, Washington, another small town in the area. Mom sent me to a private school at a church named House of the Lord, which was just across from the lot our double-wide trailer was on. I attended Sunday school there and learned biblical do's and don'ts, but going to church and Sunday school was more about playing with friends than about learning.

I had to retake first grade. I felt comfortable at this school, I connected with the other kids, and the teachers were nice and helpful. They were really great at one-on-one. My favorite teacher was Mrs. James, a little schoolteacher with motherly ways who was always ready with a hug and smile. I remember sitting in her class one day and another kid who spoke used colorful language. Mrs. James gave him a lecture and proceeded to tell the class that the next child using foul language would be punished. She assigned another kid to read a scripture out of the Bible but, of course, the word ass was in this scripture. Everyone laughed while Mrs. James added a further note that it was alright if the word was in scripture. The Bible uses very colorful language. I don't know about everyone else, but I thought to myself, "This means we can say damn, damnation, breast, etc."

I made some close friends at school. It's where, at eight-years-old, I found my first crush. He was my close friend Abigail Johnson's older brother, Chad. I believe he was every girl's first crush at our school. At my ninth birthday party, Abigail whispered something in her brother's ear. The next thing I knew I was being picked up and twirled around, then a big fat kiss plastered to my cheek. This made my day, even though all the other girls wouldn't talk to me for the rest of the day. It's amazing how we allow our emotions to control our state of being. This also shows how competitive girls are. It hurt that they wouldn't talk to me. I wanted to share my joy but instead I held my head up because it seemed like the only thing to do. I didn't like the competition but found myself often involved. There were competitions about who was whose best friend, competitions about clothes, attention, and who gets invited to whose birthday parties.

In second grade, I invited all my friends in my grade to my birthday party. I can't remember who showed up. I do remember playing a game with a prize for the winner. Months before my birthday I had begged Mom for a slinky I wanted. I was so excited because I was sure I was going to get one. I opened all my presents but it wasn't there. I was disappointed. We went to go play a game that had a prize for the winner. I can't remember what the game was. My sister Holly won, Mom gave her the prize and we all watched her open it. It was MY slinky, just one more thing to mark-up against Holly. I was so jealous!

When we're young we have no idea what we're doing. We're just growing and soaking in whatever is affecting us. We don't realize that our actions are hateful or loving. Evil does its best to soak in from the influences surrounding us. It distorts the view of the truth by our emotions and false truths we grow up believing. We learn to act out in hate from emotions caused from someone's actions.

Emotions and actions concerning my sister weren't always bad. I remember having picnics with her, flying kites, and playing dolls with her. But we were never really close. I may have been resentful about her but she had issues with me too. She told me the other day, "I would always try to get you in trouble but it always backfired, this made me angry and frustrated." Our emotions and actions kept a wedge between us that prevented us from getting close. Despite these negative emotions we loved each other. If she needed help, I would help. If she was in danger, I would get protective. We walked in between hate and love for each other because we were family.

Life spiraled out of control in my adolescence. I made destructive choices. I remember one occasion at a friend's birthday party where we ate Twinkies and tried to watch porn in her basement living room. We got caught and her mother lectured us. I felt deeply guilty. I also experienced things beyond my control that greatly affected me. One evening, at a family friend's house for dinner, all of us girls locked ourselves in a bedroom. The older ones sexually abused us younger ones. We kept our clothes on but touched each other's private parts. I had no idea that this was abuse. It was more like a game in my little head. I have no ill feeling toward these girls. I don't think they realized what they were doing either. We were all really young. But regardless, this woke a fire that I couldn't understand and that couldn't be quenched. I once tried to continue this with my sister while playing house when Mom caught us and got after us. She told us how wrong it was and it hit home hard. I felt a lot of guilt. Mom kept checking in on us for a while, but she didn't have to worry because once I felt guilt I never did it again. Experiencing this has caused me to keep a close eye on my own kids.

We moved again, to Newdock Washington and I started third grade at Newdock Grade School. This made for a very long bus ride. I have fond memories of the bus, though. Madelyn Winston was a grade higher than me and was one of my closest friends. I loved her long dark brown hair. I was so angry when she cut it shoulder length. We didn't hang out much at school but we did a lot together out of school. Her mom took us to horse riding lessons and we were in 4-H together. We had one of those connections you don't find very often. I would get jealous of her other close friendships but tried to hide it because I knew it wasn't right. She would continue to be my friend even when I did something stupid. She would stand up for me when others were mad. She never believed in God, but she knew how to really love. She only lived a mile away from our house down the river that ran past our back yard. I would walk or canoe to her house. She would ride her horse, walk, and canoe to mine. She once threw a bottle with a message and some cool colorful rocks into the river that I found and bragged about to Madelyn on the bus the next day. She was amazed that I found it but hoped it would have gone much further. I think she was glad that I found it because she told me to keep the bottle after I offered to throw it back out into the water.

Our house on the Pond Orale River was home for the next 19 years. Near our home, there were open fields and some wooded areas. Life got better. There were only five or six other houses on our road. I loved walking and running in the field, swimming in the river, and riding my bike on the dirt road. I could roam, explore, and be free. I think a happy life, a life to love, can be encouraged by a healthy living situation, animals, and space to roam. I was back to collecting animals and ended up with three female cats that all became pregnant at the same time and had babies just in a few days of each other. Each cat had a litter of about ten to thirteen kittens. We had kittens everywhere. I also talked my parents into getting some rabbits for 4-H. I decided it was cruel and mean to keep them caged so I freed them. My dad ended up shooting them because they ate my mom's plants and garden. I also found a dog that was a mix of a husky and miniature poodle. The dog looked like a miniature husky. One day, when I was going to town with my dad, it decided it wanted to go along. Dad put the dog in the back of the truck. I felt that strange feeling again, like with Cheeko, but this time I made sure I voiced my fears. Dad said, "The dog will be fine." The dog jumped out when we were flying down the road and hurt its legs. We took it back home. I was mad that Dad hadn't listened to me. I ended up staying home with it because it made the most awful sounds when I walked away. We didn't keep that dog for long. It went to a good home.

In fourth grade, I had my first official boyfriend, if you want to call it that. The funny thing is that when you're dating in grade school you go out of your way to avoid each other. I remember walking into the classroom and getting excited that he was there, but I would avoid him all day and vice versa. We eventually broke up when he decided he wanted a kiss and I didn't want to give him one. He didn't even ask me himself. He sent some friends to ask for him, and then sent the same friends to break up with me. This made me very angry. I never talked to him again. Our so-called relationship only lasted a couple of weeks, but my little self felt scarred. I can still feel some of that anger. It's amazing what can scar us when we're little. Through the brutal years of grade school, we build up walls and learn defense mechanisms that help us survive. Although they helped us endure childhood, walls and defense mechanisms can become harmful as adults, preventing us from moving forward.

Fourth grade is also the year that my good friend Abigail Johnson started school in Newdock. I remember some girls came up to me and told me that they liked my friend, that she was very funny. Abigail was a big hit, as usual. I felt awesome to be connected and close to her. I also remember being scared of losing her friendship to someone else. Going to school became a way of trying to find and keep relationships, of learning to react to emotions. Grade school can be quite brutal. As children, we haven't yet learned to bridal our tongues or actions, feeding into the world of hate even if we don't hate the other kids. Even though grade school is emotionally chaotic it helps us to learn to interact with each other. I liked being at school and being with my friends, even with all the hardships, embarrassing moments, and insecurities. I was connecting with kids at school and started to disconnect from home.

I soon had another boyfriend. This time we passed notes, the "If you love me check yes or no?" with boxes to mark. We would also play with each other on the playground. He was more like a best friend. There was a time he was gone for a couple of weeks, but I can't tell you if I missed him or not. I do remember the day he returned. We were all sitting in a group waiting for the teacher to tell us a story when I saw him across the floor. He smiled at me and my heart somersaulted with nerves, so silly. We also would sit with each other on the bus since we lived in the same direction. I really don't remember anything else. I eventually kept a grudge against this one, too. Maybe it's because he never asked me to kiss him, who knows. I wish we could have reconnected as friends somewhere through school, and that the remorse of losing this friendship would have helped me value my friends. I would have done so many things differently. But we don't learn from our past without making mistakes.

I was never choosy about my friends. I believe this is because I came from a large extended family. If we connected, then I was your friend. I didn't care what you looked like or what clothes you wore. I even wanted to be friendly to the ones I didn't connect with. From a young age, I wanted to be accepted and loved. This, in no way, had anything to do with the lack of acceptance and love from home. I had plenty of it. I believe that in my young mind I was confusing the desire of giving and turning it into wanting. Wanting to give friendship and love but in the process wanting it back. My unconditional love was starting to be a bit conditional, self-seeking, and fed by my emotional desires probably from being affected by the hurt I caused and the hurt people caused me.

On my, eleventh birthday, I invited Abigail Johnson, curly haired Linda Halls, Carol Blake with the glasses, and freckle-faced Jenny Harrison over to celebrate. I loved being around all these girls. We had fun playing dress-up. I let Abigail wear my favorite high heels, though I really wanted to wear them. When we were done, we went out to mess around. We decided to go for a walk with one of us riding a bike, my bike. Abigail and I fought over the bike, a pink ten-speed with curved handlebars. I won. I think I was still angry about the high heels. I took off down the road then turned to look behind me. I saw everyone running off away from the road, away from me. This made me sad, and I felt bad. I felt that I should have let Abigail ride the bike. I didn't want her or the others mad at me. I turned around and put the bike up. This pattern of wanting my way, getting it, and then feeling remorse when it hurt someone or turned them against me repeated itself several times through my childhood.

The rest of grade school is a blur, mixed with memories of recess, special programs with singing and dancing, and school work. I hated getting up to go to school in the morning, but loved connecting with friends, and then loved to be on the bus going home in the end. The bus is also where I started to look out the window and daydream. I daydreamed of damsels in distress, and knights in shining armor. I loved fairytales. My favorite was *The Little Mermaid*. My friends and I would jump off our dock into the river playing the little mermaid. We all had to be Ariel, so we would be twins or triplets, depending on how many friends I had over. But as we got older we played less and sunbathed more. I loved the beach life.

One summer, our church organized a potluck get-to-together at Bear Camp just a mile away from our house. There was a sauna, a deep pool, and a game room. We all ran to swim in the pool. I was swimming and doing fine. I knew how to swim. We lived on the river, and I swam a lot. Something happened about the middle of the pool. I couldn't get my legs to function right, I was kicking but I wasn't going anywhere, and I started struggling. I kept thinking, "Just keep my head above the water!" That moment when I knew I was going to go under, I saw Abigail grab her brothers' arm and point at me. Chad grabbed me and pulled me to safety. I can't really explain why I started to drown. I had no cramps in my legs, and I wasn't tired. It almost felt like someone was trying to pull me down but no one was preventing my legs from kicking. I guess it was just one of those unexplainable things that just happen or some unseen force was trying to end my life. I felt very thankful for my friend and her brother. When someone saves your life the feeling of gratitude will make you feel connected to that person. This is a form of love that says I'm thankful for your existence. You have blessed my life.

Also, in this very active year of 1988, my mom gave birth to my brother Jason. I was too busy with grade school to remember much about her pregnancy, save her big round belly. I was seeking anything that made me happy and reached for anything that made life enjoyable, learning to follow my emotions by flying with the positive and running from the negative. I was a girl trying to bloom who was very lost in her emotions. I had an eternity to walk before I would become the woman I am today. Despite my blindness to the future, I was growing slowly.

3. EMOTIONS OUT OF WHACK

*"Keep your heart with all diligence,
For out of it springs the issues of life."*
~Proverbs 4:23

    In junior high my friends and I used silly boasting to impress others and tried to outdo each other's performances. We also sought to rebel and pull away from authority and truth. With puberty came all the hormones that made everything in life extreme. My friends and I would act loud and boisterous to draw attention to ourselves. Some pre-teens would do this even individually, but not me. I had to be part of a group. At recess my friends and I would rough around to make a disturbance, create a crown of daisies for our heads, and break out into song and dance. We did all this to draw attention to ourselves and impress the opposite sex. I remember often looking around to see who was watching. This time of life isn't just about learning and growing from our actions, but about getting emotional immaturity out of our systems. It's also a time where boys and girls notice each other in different ways. I would often flirt with the boys, especially within my group of friends. I wanted to be noticed. I was also definitely noticing. I loved looking at boy's eyes. Also, friendships would come and go with highly unreasonable mental reactions. My best friend Brook and I lost our friendship from poor choices and poor reactions. Now, I look at junior high kids and think they're from another planet, that the pre-teen age is the strangest. It's where a time of acting out in hate is just the thing.
    I started to rebel against my mom, and it seemed that my mom began to change too. I became even more disconnected from my family. I wanted and felt I needed to find connections outside of the home. Kids want to cross the fence to the other side no matter what life is like at home. All kids have

a desire to be a bit like the story of the prodigal son found in Luke 15. We can definitely journey far from how we were raised during this time. It seemed to me that the grass always looked much greener on the other side. I wanted some of that grass. I wanted to be a part of new life and new adventure. I didn't want responsibilities, I wanted to break free and find relationships with excitement that were appealing to my senses, and not in a healthy way. We may have God-given desires to disconnect and leave the home. These desires are healthy and positive. I went more toward the negative. My main focus became the opposite sex and the false truths I knew about love. I believed love to be pure emotion. It was almost like a religion.

I was also attending church and youth group at Newdock Assembly of God. We no longer went to House of the Lord. I loved going to church, mainly for the fellowship by enjoying the connections with other believers my age. I loved singing songs and that singing could draw attention to myself. I also believed I was living according to the Bible. I was so deceived! I couldn't see beyond my own desires and selfishness. My emotions boxed me in. But even though they trapped me, there were times that my positive actions would lead to goodness for others. This gave me a desire to want to reach out and help people. Despite my self-centeredness, God was working in my life. Genesis 50:20 (NKJV), "But as for you, you meant evil against me; but God meant it for good, in order to bring it about as it is this day, to save many people alive." The evil that comes from us and against us, God can use for good. The curses that are sent to us or caused by us will turn to blessings when we belong to Him.

Mom started creating more responsibilities for me. She volunteered me to wear a costume for a local business. I was moving up and down the sidewalk, miserable in my outfit when two women and a young girl with down syndrome approached me. The girl came up to me, and I gave her some candy. She hugged me, and I hugged her back. I patted her head and played with her. The mother started to cry. She came over and thanked me, giving my dumb big costume head a hug. She explained that not too many people have been nice to them because of her daughter's condition. I wasn't allowed to speak in the costume so I moved my arms by waving them, then I lifted them with a shrug of my shoulders. It was hopeless. I nodded the uncomfortable head hoping this showed my understanding. I will never forget that day for as long as I live. I felt very humbled and also felt completely like me. I realized I love helping people. Whispers of truth were echoing in my soul.

I wanted to help everyone. My mom encouraged me to start babysitting the neighborhood kids. I tried to be a fun babysitter, and prove myself trustworthy to the parents. My mom taught me that I should clean and do the dishes while babysitting. I had a good reputation and parents called me back again. I once had the entire neighborhood's 13 kids at my house. It was hard for me to tell anyone no. It didn't even occur to me that this would be too many kids. I felt I had to say yes because I thought it was the right thing to do. I also wanted to please and be loved by everyone. I thought, at this time in my life, that this was a positive. I wanted to please people.

I couldn't stand firm on the word "no." I often babysat a neighbor boy. His mother went out partying on Friday and Saturday nights. She would bring men home, and he would see them French kissing. He kept bugging and bugging me to try it with him. I said fine and showed him a fake French kiss, just basically a peck moving the head from side to side. The boy told his mom. I quickly denied it and said the boy must have been dreaming. I definitely crossed a line! I felt sick to my stomach. It was heavy and turning with guilt. I was hot-faced with shame. I promised myself nothing like this would ever happen again. I learned from my mistake, but still needed to remember to forgive myself to heal so I could grow. Guilt has a down side. If guilt prevents forgiveness and letting go, then guilt will bring negativity and hate to one's self. Forgiving one's self is very important and not often done or considered. I will still be forgiving to others but forget myself. Forgiveness shows love to others and to ourselves. I was too young to understand this, but the energy of God's love was working within me.

During this time, I continued to rebel. Mom started to push more chores on me at home. She was really strict on how she wanted things done. She liked to have things perfect. No spot went undetected, no smear unseen, and nothing could be out of place. I did the dishes, weeded the garden, washed the kitchen table and floors, dusted, vacuumed, cleaned windows, and generally maintained the outdoors. If my siblings and I didn't do it right, we had to redo it all over again. I would become aggravated. I grumbled under my breath and stuck my tongue out at her while her back was turned. I disrespected and hated her while still loving her.

I can see that Mom acted in love. She wasn't against me. Mom showed her love by letting me go places, bring friends home, and throw parties with my youth group friends. She was there when I absolutely needed her. She made sure we had meals, clothes, and accessories. All of our needs were met and then some. She allowed me freedom to become who I am and to find myself. There were times I tried to act or dress a certain way that would have led me down a destructive road. I wanted to follow my friends' definition of "cool." Mom would put a stop to this. She would not allow me to become a follower. Yet I was too scared to be a leader. I was stuck in the middle. I felt caged, held back from flying by my mother. She was trying to help me fly, not hold me back. But because of my rebellion I couldn't see this. I thought she was being hateful.

My dad was always gone, working hard as a carpenter to give us a good life. He came home tired and just wanted to watch television with his family. He made sure his children wanted for nothing. I was Dad's little girl and loved to hang out with him. I always felt really close to him and I could talk to him about anything. He always listened without being judgmental and it made me feel like he cared. Dad got to play the good guy while Mom seemed like the villain. I began to love my solitude, partly because of the conflict I was having with Mom. I closed myself in my room to read books, draw, write, or just daydream. I enjoyed being in my own little world. I think all the Disney movies went a little to my head. Despite the closeness dad and I had, I grew apart from him. I wasn't only changing at home but at school too.

I wasn't hanging out with Abigail as much anymore. We both were making new friends and drifted apart, though with no ill feelings. Abigail and I had history. I knew we would always remain friends even if we weren't close anymore. She became close to the very pretty Erica Bronson, whose silky long haired and curvy older sister Ellen, was dating the handsome Chad. Chad and Ellen made the best couple in school. Abigail and Erica seemed to have one of those ideal friendships we all look for. I loved being around them both. They were both spirited and crazy. Their personalities complemented each other. Although we were drifting apart I absolutely loved it when Abigail and her family moved across the river from me. I would sometimes use my binoculars to spy on them, just for the fun of it. I canoed over there to play. We had fun competitions where Chad would try to help me win. I could see that this drove Abigail crazy. It felt like we were sisters.

In seventh grade, a new boy started at our school. I ended up liking Braden a lot. We became close and ended up dating. Dating was very different now than in grade school. It wasn't about play-dating or avoiding each other anymore. We held hands and were around each other whenever we could be. My two best friends Mary Loren and Alma More, along with Braden and his best friend James, and I were always doing things together. One afternoon we were hanging out at my house. Braden wanted a ride on my white horse Snow, who was a gift from a distant neighbor. My parents and I boarded him out not too far away. I would sometimes stake him out in the empty lot next to ours. Braden and I rode him down the road while Mary rode my bike. Mary was ahead of us, a precaution against Snow's deathly fear of bikes. Braden decided he wanted a kiss. He gave this speech of being a knight on a white horse wanting to give his girl a kiss. I think he had this planned from the beginning. I wasn't sure of doing this, but decided it wouldn't hurt to try it. It was just an extended peck. He asked if I liked it. There were no sparks and it seemed kind of gross—it definitely was not what I imagined it would be. I told him, "Not really." He shrugged his shoulders and said, "You're not ready yet." This was the beginning of the end of listening to my conscience. My emotions took over and began to rule even more.

My parents started letting me go to the movies with my friends. I would primp up for this, going through several outfits before meeting my friends there. I wanted to look my absolute best. I met Braden a couple of times, and we would sit watching films with his hand on my leg. I liked the physical touch. It made me tingle with excitement. It's no wonder we're drawn to the destructive side. It can feel so good and enticing.

Even though my dating relationship with Braden was more normal than my past relationships, we were still just kids. It's a time where a relationship becomes a crossroad between play and real. One other time Braden wanted to ride on the handlebars of the bike that I was on. We were doing fine going down the road until I lost control, went off the road, and smacked him into a tree. I never laughed so hard. It was like a cartoon with the bike coming to a dead stop when the tire hit the tree, sending Braden flying from the handlebars right smack dead center with his arms and legs spread out in a free fall theme. You would think this would be the end of our relationship but it wasn't. He laughed too after the shock wore off. Our relationship ended when he moved away. Braden may have been more of a "real boyfriend," but we were both still very immature. Like my bike losing control, my life started to speed out of control also.

I soon found another friend, Brook Rice, the best tomboy ever. We did everything together. We loved horses. We were in parades, and I tagged along with Brook and her mother, who joined the Back Countrified Horse Men, a group that did a lot of horse activities in the wilderness. We were boy-crazy and watched the musical *Newsies* all the time. My favorite was the blond-haired boy with the patch over his eye. We loved adventure. We joined the Poker Paddle Pick, canoeing 40 miles up the Pond Orale River.

One night Brook was over to stay the night. It was after dinner and we rinsed and put the dishes in the dishwasher before going to my room. My room wasn't in the house. It was out in the garage, next to the TV room. I was totally isolated out there, and I loved it. Brook and I were drawing when Mom came bursting through my bedroom door. She was yelling and screaming that I didn't do the dishes. I know I did. Flying over the top we said some ugly things. She barked that I didn't push start on the dishwasher. After Mom left I just wanted to run away. Brook said I could come live with her and her mom. I really wanted to. Mom came back and apologized. She had overreacted due to too much stress. I think her ability to admit when she's in the wrong made a huge impact on me during my whole adolescence.

Brook and I were camping with Back Countrified Horse Men when I met my first serious, soon-to-be-boyfriend. Shawn Larson, who had a strong resemblance to my blond-haired, blue-eyed *Newsie* crush, showed up to camp. I was a bit shy, but Brook wasn't. She flirted mercilessly with Shawn. His face turned red a couple of times. After that weekend we went back to ordinary life and school. I thought I would never see him again. But one morning when I was still asleep Mom brought me the phone. She tried to wake me, but she wasn't really succeeding. She got me to sit up, then handed me the phone. I stared at it. All the sudden I thought it was a snake and started beating it against the bed. Mom yelled, "Heather, stop it's Shawn!" I woke up and said a very hesitant hello. He asked me out, I said yes, and that was that. It turned out he had a class with my older cousin Haylie. He had talked about how much he liked me and Haylie, recognizing my name, gave him my number.

I connected to his mom and sister immediately. They even started going to our church. They were fun, giving, and enjoyable to be around. If I'd understood what true love was, I would have realized I loved his mom and sister a lot more than I did him. His mom made the best hot cocoa, talked forever, and was fun to listen too.

While I was very excited about my relationship with Shawn, I was losing my friendship with Brook. I was in the eighth grade now and Brook somehow got together with Mindy Henwick. Mindy was one of those girls who forced her way into popularity by making herself a leader and putting herself above others. She had to have her way and be right all the time. Even though she was considered popular, I discovered she was not well liked. She seemed to be very unforgiving and judgmental. Brook and Mindy invited me into the bathroom one day. Mindy had a bottle of alcohol on her. They both took a sip but I said, "No thank you." I thought I was trying to live righteously but I wasn't a tattle tale. I promised I wouldn't tell. Brook backed me up. We went back to class. I was so excited they trusted me that I was telling Annie Ramson all about it. I knew she wouldn't say anything, because she was just that way. She kept things to herself. But I didn't see the eavesdropper behind me. That eavesdropper, who always tattled, gave my name to the principle, and he told Brook and Mindy. In a sense, it was my fault for losing Brook's friendship. Sometimes I wished I took that drink. I got tired of being called the goody-two-shoes. But I had my principles.

I may have refused to drink, but I relaxed in other areas. Because Brook and I were no longer friends, I spent all my time with Shawn. We would find places to make out. I finally liked the kissing. He even came with me and my family to Oregon to see my extended family. My family always made a trip to Oregon in the summer to connect with other family. On one trip, my older cousin Travis, had a little puppy that fit into the palm of my hand. Travis gave her to me. She had the coloring of a Yorkie, with the dark brown fur and light brown around the eyes, ears, and paws. She was a little mutt mixed between a Yorkie and a Pug. I named her Pugzie.

When it came time for the Poker Paddle Pick it was Shawn, Pugzie and me who joined this time. I didn't have as much fun without Brook. But we did get in the newspaper labeled as the "Puppy Poker Paddle Pick." I loved that little dog so much. We did everything together. We took walks, went places, and she even slept on my bed. She was my little companion. I loved her as much as one could love an animal.

Love to me at this time was something physical and emotional. I had no understanding that it was so much more. My attraction and relationship to Shawn was very physical. My downfall was not alcohol or drugs but the sensation behind a passionate touch: lust. I am not proud of my relationship with Shawn. He was the first step onto a road of destruction. I kept telling myself that I was doing nothing wrong if I didn't allow it to get carried away, that it was alright as long as we didn't go all the way. One night while making out, he took my virginity with his fingers. I didn't even know what happened. I thought I had just started my period until I read a book that was not meant for girls my age to read a couple days later in which a girl lost her virginity. I still chose to believe that I was alright because I didn't go all the way. I didn't want to know or face the truth. Every time I started to feel guilt I would tell myself that I wasn't doing anything wrong. For the first time, I ignored that guilty feeling. I chose to believe a lie that put me under bondage. Living in denial doesn't fix the issue. This is where guilt can destroy. I chose to let it fester. Because I chose not to listen I fell further down the road of destruction.

Even though we had some good times our relationship was not a healthy one. Shawn would always break up with me because of something I did that he didn't like. He played head games to trick me into doing what he wanted me to do. I heard from his sister that he became angry at his mom one night and flipped the kitchen table. None of these things occurred to me as bad signs. I thought our relationship was perfect. I thought he was the man I was going to marry. I was so young and naive. Our relationship lasted for about three years until I got tired of the games and broke it off. He tried to get me back, but I was completely over him. He didn't have a chance.

I used to picture love as a young woman catching her breath while a young man stands in front of her. He slowly takes her hands with a light touch. Tingles rush up their arms. Their eyes meet while they become light-headed with love for each other. The mists sitting heavily around them make them feel they are the only ones who exist. The young man slowly bends his head and touches his lips to hers. At that moment with all her being, her heart instantly becomes his.

I, an impressionable young female just blooming into a young woman, got caught up in the passions of her first love. It didn't matter if my home life was complete or not. I wanted that fairytale type of love and romance. I watched all the movies, listened to the love songs, and read the books. I would even sneak adult romance books if I could, though I did sometimes try to skip the sex scenes. I was a bit infatuated with it all. Imagine my surprise when I found some of the best love stories in the Bible, and also, some great poetic love scenes. I couldn't believe it when I found a chapter that speaks about breasts, and reading it as a parable, its meaning becomes so much more. I couldn't stop laughing when I read it. I can picture people probably thinking, "I can't believe she's talking about breasts!" At my young age, I found it very funny to see the word breast in the Bible, giggling as a 16-year-old while reading sections of Song of Solomon as I sat in the back pew in church.

This time of my life brought great change from adolescents to a form of young adulthood. Even though I wanted to be friendly to everyone, I wanted to find those I would really connect with. The girls who I connected to best were tomboys, probably as a result of my childhood at the cabin with my cousins. Everyone was hitting puberty at this time, wanting to rebel, and encouraging each other in rebellion. We were all giving into our emotions from the highs and lows. This was a time of difficult change between family and friends.

4. HITTING BOTTOM

"Do not be deceived, God is not mocked; for whatever a man sows, that he will also reap.
For he who sows to his flesh will of the flesh reap corruption, but he who sows to the Spirit will of the Spirit reap everlasting life."
~Galatians 6:7-8

When I was 16 I had a car that broke down on me too many times to count. I had no boyfriend, though I was looking. Life didn't seem complete if I didn't have a boyfriend. I was a girl spiraling back and forth, trying to be good and then getting tired of being good. It seemed that evil and good kept playing tug-of-war with me. I was more involved with church and youth group at this age. We had a large fun youth group. Our pastor and youth leader were always breathing excitement into our gatherings. They always had fun games to play like who could jump across the most chairs. They always, somehow, would use these games as a life lesson from scripture. They knew how to draw in teenage kids. For them this was truly a gift. My church felt like a second home. This was all great, but in reality, the youth group was just another way to connect with more friends and flirt with other boys. Yes, my prayers were true, my praise and worship came from the heart, but listening to scripture was about half and half. I was more interested in what I wanted, not what was right in the eyes of God. I believed that what I wanted was what God wanted, a very common lie. I believed my emotions, the good ones, tied into the desires of God. What I didn't realize was that some emotions, though they feel good, are negative, even hateful. I couldn't see that all these negative emotions were consuming me.

Underneath all the smiley faces and good intentions lived jealousies, bitterness, hatred, and many more negative feelings. My sister and I would fight over who got to be Linda Mirell's friend. Of course, we couldn't share, that was unheard of. She was younger than me but older than Holly. She had beautiful long blond hair, a gorgeous face, and a voice that moved your soul. If this girl chose to make it in the musical world she would have gone far. I loved her and hated her. I enjoyed being her friend, but also looked at her with green-eyed envy. I was all mixed up.

I also started to become more of a leader, at least behind the scenes. If I was on the worship team I had to be a backup singer. I would freeze with stage fright if I was put as the lead singer. Linda, on the other hand, could lead worship very well. I loved to try harmonizing with her. Our youth group did many functions such as all-nighters at the church, car washes, and Jesus Northwest—a huge concert in the Northwest where many Christian musicians get together to perform. My family also became good friends with the pastor and his family. Pastor Kenneth and his wife Shelly were the type of people who instantly made you feel like part of the family. They were open, accepting, and caring. Their sons became good friends with my brothers. Our families had a lot of get-togethers. Somewhere in the middle of all this they had a male friend who came to stay with them from Denver. Daren was three or four years older than me. I fell for him, and we started dating. He was so different from the boys in the area. He was older and, I believed, more mature. He had to be the one, right?

Daren had to go back home so we decided to try long distance dating. We would call and talk to each other quite often. One summer he moved in with Pastor Kenneth and became our youth group leader. We found ourselves in a bit of a predicament, because I was part of the youth group. As a youth group leader, it wasn't right for him to date a youth group member. We backed off a little and tried to hide the fact we were dating. He would often show favoritism to Linda, which drove me crazy mainly because there was already a jealousy issue there. I would let my negative emotions get the better of me and I would have an attitude toward him and her afterwards. I found it hard to get over my frustrations. But this didn't last long. He moved back to Denver, stopped communicating, and broke up.

Meanwhile at school, Jared Jerome started to like me. He was easy on the eyes and any girl would be lucky to have him. He asked me out. I said yes and broke up with him a week later. I was still hung up on Daren. I explained that it wasn't fair to him but I would like to still be friends. He was alright with this. He wanted to have lunch with me out in his truck that afternoon but I forgot all about it. This was the end of our friendship. I had never felt so bad. He was one of those nice guys that would do anything for someone. He did not deserve a hurt heart. My heart was just not into this relationship.

A few weeks after, Daren called. We started dating long distance again. He invited me to come stay a week with him in Denver the next summer. I'm surprised my parents let me. When I got off the plane he met me with a rose.

I took it and gave him a hug. I hung my rose up to dry when we got to his dad's house. I liked drying flowers because then they would last forever. I soon found out Daren was not a very good host. I had no knowledge of the area but he forced me to choose activities to plan. He took me to a drive-in theater, where we made out more than we watched. He then took me to see his sister, and later his cousins. I really liked them. We did things with them as a group. I had a really good time with them, but I was not too impressed with Daren. I knew that this would be the end of us. He was really temperamental. I suppose I was too, but I couldn't see past the end of my nose.

Soon the visit was over and I was back at the airport saying goodbye. I was happy to be going home. I still had my rose with me. I set it next to my seat in the groove against the wall. When I was close to home, I picked up the rose and noticed something was different about it. It molded. There was hairy mold on my rose! I had never seen one do this. I took this as a sign that my relationship with Daren was moldy. It was definitely over.

I was back home, back to life and high school, day in and day out. I had many friends but was not what you considered popular. I did not stay in clicks though I was considered religious. I had friends in every click from the popular, religious (any religion), the druggies, the grungies, and to the nerds. I tried to be nice to everyone. The only thing that really got to me was when people labelled me as a goody-two-shoe. I was not. I had my own set of problems. I was not interested in drugs or alcohol; they were not my downfall. But, I was tired of this title, and I decided to see why everyone thought getting drunk was such great fun. Drugs were out of question! I decided to get plastered with my friend Blair, who I met at church and was also living with us at the time. Holly was in on it too. Dad and Mom were gone for the weekend and a friend of Blair's got us some booze. We drank the night away with the hard alcohol. We were dumb and goofy. It was nearing dawn when I decided I was hungry so we went out to eat. I skipped having a hangover for some unexplainable reason. I got lucky. But even with that luck I couldn't and still can't understand why people like being drunk. I had a better time being sober. That was my first and last time. So, I just kept that title. If people were going to like me, they were going to like me for who I was. There were some who didn't much care for me, especially Mindy. She still held a grudge about being found out when drinking in the bathroom.

The eavesdropper who tattled on Mindy, Helen, worked hard to be the teacher's pet, and she would always tattletale. She was also in every function and sport she could participate in. Her father was a coach and math teacher, who I really liked. Her mother was a coach and P.E. teacher, and was not someone you wanted to cross. Everyone liked her younger sister. Helen was not liked by quite a few people. I was one who didn't much care for her because I felt she was responsible for my falling out with Brook. My feelings changed one summer when I was entered in a horse show with my friend Madelyn. I didn't have the best looking or best behaved horse. Snow was all white with some scars, and he was a little obstinate. I was in the competition just for fun. I watched Helen win first place a few times and second place once. She was doing really well. Snow and I were walking past Helen's horse trailer when I heard yelling. I looked over and saw her mom berating her for getting second place. I was dumbfounded. I understood now why Helen tried so hard to be who she was. She desired to please her mom, who obviously was hard to please. My heart went out to her. She was trying so hard, even if it meant making enemies. I no longer held my grudge against her. I started to learn that people often act out from hurts and desires stemming from past pain.

One day, after changing out of my P.E. clothes, I was walking away from the lockers when I heard raised voices. I looked toward the entrance and office door. Mindy was bullying Helen. She was getting in Helen's face and calling her names, making a big show of it. Everyone was standing around watching, uneasy. Helen was trying to avert her eyes and ignore Mindy. You could tell no one was going to put a stop to it. My irritation rose and I walked over and told Mindy that it was enough. This turned her on me. She tried to set me off. She was looking for a fight, but she wasn't going to get one from me. I wasn't giving her any comebacks to bite on. Then she just raised her back up and yelled, "You think I'm a b****, just call me a b**** Heather, just call me a b****!" So, I said, "Fine, if that's what you want, you're a b**** Mindy." But of course, just as this came out of my mouth our P.E. teacher, Helen's mom, opened the office door with the look of surprise blooming on her face. I was known to never curse. It wasn't who I was. All the girls left immediately. I was going to stay and apologize and explain but Helen beat me to it. Her mom let it go. After school Mindy convinced a bunch of cheerleaders to surround me as I stood talking with someone. I had no clue they were there because I was wrapped up into my conversation. I only noticed them after I got on the bus and sat down. The next day a few girls came up to me and apologized for their part in it. They had no idea it was me. If they had known it was me, they wouldn't have gotten involved in Mindy's plan to come after me. This showed me that Mindy was prone to manipulation and deception. She could hate me all she wanted, but at least I knew I was standing up for what was right. I was being real with myself, in this situation at least. After all this, while in youth group, our youth pastor was speaking on forgiveness and asking for forgiveness from those we didn't think we really wronged. I thought of Mindy. I may or may not have done anything wrong, but she felt wronged. I decided to apologize to Mindy. I caught her one morning before we were in the school building.

I yelled, "Hey Mindy!" to get her attention. She came over and I apologized. "I'm sorry for the way I wronged you and have treated you." She nodded then replied, "Can I ask you one thing? Were you the one that told on Brook and I in junior high?" I told her, "No, I didn't tell on you." She wanted to know who did. Given the history of Mindy and Helen I thought it best she didn't know. I looked at her and said, "I honestly did not tell on you but I can't tell you who did." We never had any problems after this, but we weren't close either. Forgiveness, no matter who's at fault, brings healing.

I may have been real on some aspects of life but when it came to boys I was fooling myself. Garret Morel was very attractive with fascinating blue eyes, and he was fun to be around, or so I thought. I just had one issue. My friend, Missy, chased after him for quite a while. I kept my feelings and my attraction to myself. Missy really had the hots for him. Our other mutual friend Nicky was trying to help Missy make it happen. So, he was off limits, right? He walked me to the bus one day after school and we stood talking by the door of the bus. He was trying to find out who I liked. I wouldn't tell. He was going off on how he was so tired of Missy chasing after him. I just gave a little smile. Then he was begging, "Please tell me who you like?" I thought, "Fine! Who could it hurt? Nothing will come of it anyways." He was just a friend. The bus driver was about to close the bus doors so I blurted out, "you!" and climbed into the bus. He said the next day, that he liked me too. I wonder now if it was just a ploy to get Missy off his back. Against my better judgment we started dating.

Making this choice caused me to lose a really good friend. I betrayed her. I was not at all proud of this. But I was addicted to relationships like one becomes addicted to drugs. They became more important than friendships. I wish my older self could go back and slap some sense into my younger self. Like all my relationships we made out. Garret and I did everything under the sun but the actual act of sex. Our relationship only lasted for a couple of months, with Missy and Nicky trying everything to break us up. I'm not sure if it was them or Garret himself, thinking he didn't need me anymore, that caused our end. Whoever it was, this breakup had a bad ending for me. I wasn't really heartbroken, more upset that I lost a friend over something that didn't last. It was a hard lesson to learn and an expensive one. I lost a bit of myself in the process. This caused me to backtrack and take a hard, long, deep look into myself.

After the breakup, I was walking down the hallway at school, getting back into a lonesome routine, when a guy who I always thought was cute walked up to me. He had the nerve to offer to pay me to make out with him. I was shocked! He then further explained that Garret was telling everything we did to everyone. I became very embarrassed. I heard someone say, "Garret that's enough, this is going too far!" I looked over and saw a lot of people standing and sitting around. I saw my good friend, a tall blond named Dick Webler, who to this day remains dear to my heart. He stood up for me. I also saw Jared Jerome, Missy, and Nicky encouraging Garret to tell all. I really couldn't blame them. But it hurt. It was agonizing. I looked at the guy who offered to pay me and said "NO!" I became very bitter over this. It was so hard to face everybody at school for the next couple of weeks. Dick asked me out probably just wanting to cheer me up. Dating was completely different with him. He didn't try anything. I loved him for that. I was still riding the negative emotional wave over what Garret did. We broke up as friends a week later and stayed good friends. It was almost like he just wanted to take my hand and just walk with me a little way in order to mend my wings so I wasn't afraid to fly again.

In this time of my life, being dumped and humiliated by Garret shoved me down hard. It was my version of hitting a tree, coming to a dead stop and smashing into it, but this time I wasn't laughing. I started to evaluate who I was and what I'd become. I focused less on what I thought I needed and began to search for what would bring me wholeness in my spirituality. I always thought love was physical and emotional. All our emotions in love are not always truth and all the "feel good" sensations are not always positive. I was in a fog about the truth but I knew that I wanted to search for the truth about love and the man meant for me. This is a very heavy weight for a 16 or 17-year-old to hold. I remember thinking that I could let this get the better of me or I could stand tall and learn from this experience. It was the first time I thought that even though I feared life pushing me forward, or being hurt by negative actions caused by myself or others, I needed to adapt and move forward. All my rebelling, bad choices, and denial up to this point brought knowledge and wisdom through my choice to learn from my mistakes. It was just the beginning of a very long road. I was beginning to see this concept in my mind, but I didn't understand it to the fullest. I was also beginning to understand that when I follow my desires, I do not truly love myself. When I make negative choices even though they feel good, I hate myself. James 1:5-8 (NKJV) – "If any of you lacks wisdom, let him ask of God, who gives to all liberally and without reproach, and it will be given to him. But let him ask in faith, with no doubting, for he who doubts is like a wave of the sea driven and tossed by the wind. For let not that man suppose that he will receive anything from the Lord; he is a double-minded man, unstable in all his ways." My past is definitely filled with wind tossing and double-mindedness.

What female does not like romance—or the idea of it, with all the good feelings and emotions that surround it. Feeling special and important to someone, I think, is what we all look for in a relationship. I still want to feel important to my husband. I believe that it's important and healthy to make each other feel that way. We can lose sight of making them feel special and important in our selfishness and greed of what we want out of a relationship. We get so involved with taking that we forget to give.

All the bad in my life brought me to a place of deep searching where I am trying to figure out how to rise above and move forward. Even after hitting bottom brought me to a crossing, I was still confused and longed for someone to complete me. Instead of filling that God-shaped hole with God's love I was trying to fill it with worldly love. I continued to go to church and youth group. I prayed for guidance and understanding and for the man meant for me. I prayed for God's will in my life and rebuked temptations.

5. HEAVENLY INTERVENTION

"For it is written: 'He shall give His angels charge over you, to keep you,' and, 'In their hands they shall bear you up, lest you dash your foot against a stone.'"
~Luke 4:10-11

Last night sleeping in bed next to my husband, I had a dream where I was standing in the center of a black tornado. Its cloudy fog swirling around me sucking out the air so I couldn't breathe. Satan's face appeared in the cloud and laughed. I cried out, "Jesus!" A hand reached for me, grabbed my arm, and then pulled me up out of the tornado and onto a platform where I was gently set down. I looked up and Jesus stood before me. I watched as he turned and pointed to two bright angels with swords and then He pointed to where Satan was attacking me. The angels grabbed their swords and flew down for battle. I then woke from this dream knowing in my soul that God is fighting my battle for me. With all the issues, struggles, and chaos I face today I now know that God is with me. He always was, is, and will be.

During my first winter as a licensed driver, I was nervous to drive on the icy, curvy, 12 miles of road from home to Newdock. I was still soul-searching, seeking to find who I was, when my friend Dick Webler invited Blair and me over to his place for the night to hang out and play some games. I told him I would be there after work. Mom found me a job as a cleaning girl, at the same business where I wore the costume and met the Down syndrome kid. It only took me a couple of hours to clean all the offices.

You should know I'm a daydreamer. Once, I was taking my dishes to the sink I lost myself along the way daydreaming and ended up in the washroom. I recently put a tube of toothpaste in the fridge. My imagination was always causing me to think of real and non-real things. When I pictured myself rolling my mom's car and Dick driving by soon after and picking me up, I laughed. What were the chances of that happening? This was one of those daydreams that popped into my head out of nowhere. It seemed very real. I told myself that I needed to get my thoughts in control, and I went to get ready for work.

My car was in the shop again, and Mom was allowing me to use her minivan. I went to get the keys from her. She told me, "be careful!" and gave me some food to drop off for Dad, who was working on building a home a couple miles down the road along my way. Dad thanked me when I dropped off his food. He gave me a hug and looked me in the eyes telling me, "be careful, these roads are slick." I said, "I will, I'll go slowly." I knew I had to be careful. Even without my daydream and my parents loving advice, I understood the dangers. I got back into the van and was off again.

Everything was fine. The roads weren't too bad. I was driving about 10 to 15 miles under the speed limit, trying to take it slow while being careful. I came to a sharp sloping corner that was covered with shade by the trees. I started to feel the van go sideways. I had hit black ice. The front of the car was heading into a bank of snow. I turned the tires away from the turn thinking I just might spin this out. This wasn't going to happen. I knew the nose of the car was going to hit that bank. I covered my head with my arms and bent into a fetal position. The van impacted with a jerk and flipped three or four times. I was jerked around and around. I felt my head hit the side window and the window shattered. I was thrown up and down and my head hit the windshield. It all seemed to take place in slow motion. All the sudden there was dead silence. I landed with the van right side up. I was stunned and couldn't move or think. I noticed the head shaped imprint in the windshield and the shattered window next to me. I had to get out. The door didn't open. I fought with the seatbelt buckle getting loose then hunched up on the seat. I jumped out of the broken window. The back end of the van was hanging over the cliff with water below. There were trees to block a fall, but it was still scary. It all hit me hard. Within an instant a bunch of curse words come flying uncontrollably out of my mouth. Once I said the GD word I felt guilt for my outburst. I should have been thanking God for still being alive, not cursing out of frustration and fear. I repented and asked for forgiveness. I promised not to curse again. After standing next to the road being unsure on what I should do next, I instantly thought about my daydream or vision. Acts 2:17(NKJV) – "And it shall come to pass in the last days, says God, That I will pour out of My Spirit on all flesh; Your sons and your daughters shall prophesy, Your young men shall see visions, Your old men shall dream dreams."

I know it says young men will see visions, and this might confuse some, but God says He will pour his spirit on all flesh. I am a daughter of man and a daughter of God. When we choose to be in God's family we are blessed by these gifts. My vision was real. This wreck occurred exactly as I saw it in my so-called daydream. I thought of Dick picking me up. No, that couldn't happen. I saw him drive by. "NO way!" He screeched to a stop and backed up. I felt a bit dazed.

It turned out Dick just picked up a mutual friend of ours to bring to his house. Randy lived a few miles past me. Dick pointed out that I had a prick at the tip of my nose. But other than that, I was fine. I should have been bloody and mangled. But God and heaven intervened. Dick drove to the nearest house so I could call my mom. It would have been nice if cell phones were invented then. It was very strange going to a stranger's house just to use a phone. The man acted like we were criminals. Once I got Mom on the phone she asked, "Do you need to go to the hospital?" I told her, "I just want to come home!" As we left, Randy jumped in behind the passenger side seat allowing me to sit in the front of Dick's crew cab pickup. I was headed home. Both guys were talking, trying to keep me active and focused. Dick kept a good eye on me, making sure I was all right. I dropped into unconsciousness for a second. He decided to turn around and take me to the hospital. They made me talk all the way there to keep me conscious. I remember feeling like I just wanted to sleep.

When we were at the hospital we walked in, straight to the desk and explained what happened. A nurse took me to a room where she had me lay down while she asked me questions and took my pulse. I started to shake. I felt like I was having a seizure. It was the most annoying thing in the world. As I was starting to fear something was wrong with me, my dad came in. He came over, took my hand and asked, "How are you doing?" Right at that moment I wasn't too sure. Next, a doctor came in, examined me while asking more questions. With chattering teeth I asked him, "Why am I shaking so much?" He answered, saying the shaking was a response to nerves and adrenaline. A police officer came to take a report on what happened, asking me even more questions. I just wanted to go home. The doctor came back and said, "You check out clear!" I was free to leave. I said bye to Dick and Randy who stayed to make sure I was alright, and I thanked them. You couldn't ask for better friends.

Dad and I drove home. I felt completely exhausted. It was comforting to have my dad there. I became a little nervous when we pulled into the driveway of our home. I wasn't sure how to approach mom. Then mom came out. I walked toward her and started to cry, "I'm so sorry! I didn't mean to wreck the van!" She hugged me saying, "I'm just happy that you're alright." She didn't care about materialistic things. They can always be replaced. She made me smile when she explained, "I've been bugging your dad for a new car, although I didn't want to get it this way at all." At least something good came from this. Mom was able to get her new car.

The Sunday after my wreck we went to church. Things were getting back to normal. The effects of the wreck were losing its edge although I was still amazed by my vision. I was walking into the sanctuary of the church from the reception area when Shawn's mom, Annie, approached me. She gave me a hug and asked, "How are you doing?" I told her, "I'm doing fine." She looked at me hard saying, "I had the strongest urge to pray for you the other day." I asked her, "what day?" She answered. It was the same day I had my wreck. Up until all this I had struggled with doubts off and on about my beliefs. I have heard miraculous stories from others about others, and I would wonder if they were true or not. It's quite another story when heavenly interventions happen personally.

This intervention gave me chills, the good kind of chills. God and his angels were looking out for me that day. Now I see that He was looking out for me for a long time. Twice I almost drowned, and now this wreck. God was with me in spirit through the first two, but with the wreck He intervened with the host of heaven to save my life. I started to wonder, "why?" I can't say if this wreck happened to grab my attention, because I started to wander over to the road of destruction again, or if it was just because it wasn't my time yet. Regardless of the reason of this wreck and miracle, it did get me back on the right path again. Having something drastic happen to me started me thinking, "What was I meant for, what was His will for my life?" I had no clue. Jeremiah 29:11 (NKJV) – "For I know the thoughts that I think toward you, says the Lord, thoughts of peace and not of evil, to give you a future and a hope." My search continued. I decided to fly in the right direction. This little bird was tired of flying through fiery flames. I wanted to follow the light of truth.

6. BREAKING FREE

"Stand fast therefore in the liberty by which Christ has made us free, and do not be entangled again with a yoke of bondage."
~Galatians 5:1

During my sophomore and junior years, I used to cover my walls with a collage of pictures cut from teen magazines. Instead of a Facebook feed, I had a wall feed. It fed by basic desires. I had everything up there that was interesting to my fleshly self. I taped up worldly images of what a girl should be in physical looks and clothing. I also had pictures of the guys I was infatuated with and quotes about dating as a teen. I enjoyed taping them up, even on my bedroom door. But one morning I woke up unhappy with them. I realized that this was not who I was meant to be. I tore them down. This made me feel good, giving me a form of release. When they were all down and my walls were empty, I felt refreshed. I pictured myself as my wall covered with stuff. All those fleshly forces were blocking the true me. I had all this junk blocking my view of what was real. It's very easy to fall into the lies of the flesh. Paul wrote in Romans 7: 15-25 "For what I am doing, I do not understand. For what I will to do, that I do not practice; but what I hate, that I do. If, then, I do what I will not to do, I agree with the law that it is good. But now, it is no longer I who do it, but sin that dwells in me. For I know that in me (that is, in my flesh) nothing good dwells; for to will is present with me, but how to perform what is good I do not find. For the good that I will to do, I do not do; but the evil that I will not to do, that I practice. Now if I do what I will not to do, it is no longer I who do it, but sin that dwells in me. I find then a law, that evil is present with me, the one who wills to do good. For I delight in the law of God according to the inward man. But I see another law in my members warring against my mind, and bringing me into captivity to the law of sin which is in my members. O wretched man that I am! Who will deliver me from this body of death? I thank God- through Jesus Christ our Lord. So then, with the mind I myself serve the law of God, but with the flesh the law of sin."

Taking the clips off the wall was just the beginning of finding myself and understanding freedom. I still wanted to discover true love and the man that would fill my desires. I was heavily involved in church and youth group. It was becoming more important than school. I loved God, but I still had an overwhelming need to find my soul mate. Instead of getting interested in boys at school, I was looking elsewhere. I wanted to find one who held the same beliefs as I did. Somehow, I came across the book, *Romance God's Way*, by Eric Ludy. This book was a turning point to my life. It spoke to my heart and made me long for God's choice and timing for my soulmate. Right then and there, alone in my bedroom, I prayed for Gods direction for my life and for someone who was meant for me. I prayed, "Lord forgive me for sins I've committed with the belief of needing a boyfriend. For the fleshly desires that were stirred in me and awakened. I repent and ask for your healing and guidance. Give me the desire to wait upon you, your timing, and the one you have for me, in the name of Jesus." I no longer felt lead by my physical desire to need someone. I stopped looking for a boyfriend! I was free from the desires that trapped me into believing that I needed to have a boyfriend.

My church scheduled a day for baptism and I decided to get baptized. I was changing in so many ways. I wanted to wash my old self away. I desired to start this journey new and refreshed as it was a new beginning, a new me. When it came to my turn I walked up onto the stage to the little pool behind the pulpit. I was so nervous. Everyone was watching. I pretended it was just me and the pastor. We stood in the water together. He said his speech then asked me why I wanted to be baptized. I said, in a quiet, shy voice, "I want God to be my center. I want to be a new creation in Him."

My pastor dunked me and quickly said the baptismal prayer, "I baptize you in the name of the Father, Son, and Holy Ghost!" I was lifted out. This all happened so fast but when I came out from under the water I truly felt new. So much weight was lifted off my shoulders. I literally felt as though I was walking on clouds. I have no idea what other people experience after their baptism. I have never heard anyone talk about it. I felt like a new creation.

As I was seeking to be closer to God, my drawings, paintings, and writing were leaning more toward the spiritual side. Instead of dragons and fairytale people I was creating pictures of the soul and spirit. My writings went from comedy animal stories to short stories of spiritual matters. I often wrote these stories in biology class, probably one of the reasons I failed it twice. I disliked science—not just because of the evolution theory—but because I had no interest in it. I hated all the long difficult words and terms. Here is one of my early stories from biology class. I have left it in its original, unedited form to give an idea of who I was at the time, as well as my early writing.

The Crown

"A woman sees a crown sitting next to the throne of God. It's a gift that he has given from the depths of his love. She takes it into her hands and places it on her head. She turns and walks away. The Lord sheds a tear for her mistake. For letting her stubbornness and pride to overcome the Lord's will for her life. How his heart cries out to her . . . but, she cannot hear. She's too consumed pleasing the world. Years have passed since the day that she turned away. Her fire has died and her heart is filled with pain and sorrow. The smile from her face has faded. She can't understand the turn her life has taken. Yes . . . she still believes in Jesus, but, she doesn't understand why He's been so silent. And she can't feel the deepness of his love. She lies on her bed shedding rivers of tears in her pillow. Beaten and broken from the world she so poured her flesh. The Lord wraps his arms around her tenderly. He whispers in her ear comforting words to sooth her pain. His love washes over her. She remembers that crown that she so selfishly had taken. Her soul runs back to Him, she falls before His thrown taking the crown from her head and placing it at His feet. Tears of healing overflow her uncontrollably. His voice she can finally hear and his love relights the fire inside. Once again she is made whole. She gets off her bed and wipes the tears from her sparkling eyes. The joy has been restored ever so abundantly. She offers up thanksgiving and praise for the brokenness that has brought her back."

I'm amazed by this story. When I wrote that short story I had no idea I was writing about myself. It was just something that bubbled up from the depths of my soul. But I see it clearly now as I reread it.

Sin is a constant battle, and as life continued I started to feel weighed down by all the sin in my life. Although I conquered one area in my life I was still learning and growing. I still had other areas that needed to be conquered. There were more storms to pass through. Just because I broke free from one area doesn't mean that I was wholly cured. To be completely free takes a lot of healing in all areas of life, even areas from the past that could be hidden.

7. SEEKING TRUTH

"For everyone who asks receives, and he who seeks finds, and to him who knocks it will be opened."
~Luke 11:10 (NKJV)

    Seeking truth and understanding it is not easy, it takes time and learned lessons throughout the course of life. I went from one extreme to another. I jumped from ice to fire. No happy medium for me. Finding truth is a lifelong journey. There's always something to learn.

    I did not feel connected to school my senior year. School was no longer the center of my life. I felt like a robot walking through my classes. If I had the option to home school like I do with my children I probably would have taken that road. Dad wasn't around much. Mom and I were growing further apart. Holly and I never really connected, and my brothers were young and being boys. I felt like I had to search, find who I was, and discover a place in this world where I belonged. I had no idea where I fit. I was trying hard to walk the right path while I was seeking truth and a future.

    We need all seasons to be healthy and grow. I now see and understand that we are all at different stages of life walking our own personal journeys. My own journey was slowly moving along. I wasn't done just because I broke free of a single bondage. There are many little battles in a war. But I was moving forward. I went through a discipleship class that was taught by a lady from Newdock Assembly of God. In this class I earned a discipleship certificate. This was one of the last main functions I did at this church. This class taught me how to interact with others and how to communicate with love.

    I left the Newdock Assembly of God, and without my family I decided to go back to House of the Lord. I heard that the youth group there was a good one. My goofy friend Linda encouraged me to come check it out. I loved it. I clicked and felt a connection so I started going there. It helped that House of the Lord's youth group was basically a young adult group. A lot of older people were there. This youth group became a family to me. I made a best friend for life named Jennie, we became just as close as Brook and I used to be. It was great to be close to someone again.

My life was moving along and I did my best to do what I thought was right. I struggled with the weight of what was right or wrong. I kept getting them mixed up. My Aunt Betty had a friend at work who was trying to find her nephew or son, I can't remember, a date. Yes, my aunt set me up with a blind date. I told her that I didn't date anymore. Aunt Betty begged and begged, "Please, please! I told my friend you would." I said, "Fine!" I decided I could just go but nothing was going to come of it—and I wasn't going alone. So, a double blind date was set up. I really didn't want to go!

He, Clyde, brought his cousin Trevor, and I brought my friend Mary. I was irritated, but polite. Clyde and Mary hit it off. His cousin, Trevor, was really fun. But I didn't want a relationship. So, when the date was over we planned another get-together so Clyde and Mary could go as a couple. On the second date, I drove Mary's car around while Mary and Clyde sat in the back. We didn't know what to do. I didn't want to be there. I wanted to be at youth group, which was that night. We were in Friar River, coming back to Newdock on the Old Friar River's curvy road, the back way from town to town. I suggested, "Why don't we go to youth group? It's a great youth group!" Trevor was up for it, and the other two reluctantly agreed. The church was not that far from where we were. Everyone was happy to see us and welcomed the new people I brought with enthusiasm. I was just glad I could make it.

Our youth group was a bit unorthodox. It wasn't just sitting and listening to someone who preaches on and on. We all were involved. It was like a big come-over-slumber-party. We played guess games from scripture. We would all take the opportunity to stand up and share from our hearts and relay scripture that touched our lives. We also had a blast putting on skits and joked around. We had times of prayer where anyone could chime in. Our youth pastor wasn't the kind that stood above us. He was part of us. There was a lot of love in this youth group, a lot of openness, and very little judgment. We were family and very open to the guests. Trevor had a great time. He thanked me for bringing him and said, "I'll be back next week!" He became a big part of this youth group and we became great friends. He told me that he had been about to give up on God. I think God had this planned from the very beginning. This time he willed me into being a servant for someone else. I felt blessed to be a part of Gods plan for this young man's life.

I now see that I was being a bit closed off in my limited and normal way of viewing God's will. God was working in my life even when I was refusing the blind date Aunt Betty committed me too. I was blind to what God wanted, but thought I was doing what God wanted. There is a healthy way to date and an unhealthy way to have a boyfriend. I was still learning. I had moved from one extreme to the other. As God was paving a way for me I was zigzagging from one side of the road to the other trying to find the right place to be, and I still do this.

I found that it was much nicer just being friends with guys, to being myself and having some brother-sister relationships. This youth group gave this to me. There was more meaning in the relationship than dating for physical contact. There were no mind games, no destructive emotions. It was real. I had a family I could connect with. I loved and will always love my parents and siblings, but it seemed that I was being pulled from one to the other.

Graduation day came and I still had no idea what direction I wanted to take. I continued to work at Safeway. The thing I wanted most was to find a man and create a family. I was always on the lookout for the one meant for me. One evening I was pushing carts in through the doors when my old pastor Kenneth from Newdock Assembly of God came up behind me. I was happy to see him. I always enjoyed his upbeat company. But he was on a mission. Daren was up from Denver visiting and sent this poor pastor in to propose marriage to me.

Pastor Kenneth timidly confronted me, "I have someone in the car who wants to propose to you but is too scared to approach you."

"Who?" I asked.

"Daren." I felt the same way I did in grade school, when my "boyfriend" sent his friends to ask for a kiss. I figured if he really wanted to marry me he should have been able to tough it out and ask me himself. I also recalled the moldy rose.

"I won't marry Daren," I told Pastor Kenneth. "I no longer have feelings for him."

Pastor Kenneth left to break the news to Daren, and I finished cleaning up the shopping carts.

Even though I was on the lookout for a man I wasn't going to jump at the first opportunity. I was looking for the moment when it felt just right. Having a pastor ask while the guy waited in the car was not right. Though I was on the road to find truth and love I was at the height of my young adult life. I was having a blast with my friends, youth group, and church. After every youth group function, we would all go to McDonalds for a late dinner, not wanting to break up the comradery of the night. We filled the restaurant. We were loud and noisy but respectful. I'm sure we were a sight to see. I enjoyed connecting with boys as friends and hoping to find a boy that would turn into something more. I do miss those days.

I formed a connection to a couple of godly women, who helped me grow spiritually. They taught me what it was to be a woman, mother, and wife. One of these women taught a purity class. I took a purity oath. Despite my past I was seeking to be pure. I was still a virgin to the real act of sexual intercourse. I wanted to learn and seek all truth in purity. She taught us that we all have someone out there meant for us. She encouraged us to write down the qualifications we would want in a husband. I don't remember everything I wrote, but I do remember writing "old-fashioned." I wish I would have specified how old-fashioned. She also taught us the right guy could become the wrong guy, and the wrong guy could become the right guy. I was so lost. I didn't understand what she meant by this. She even said that we might not understand until later on down the road.

She was right. I later figured out that it's our determination in making something work, our choices and actions that breathe life or death into a relationship. As Moses tells the Israelites in Deuteronomy 30:19, we all have the choice between life and death: "I call heaven and earth as witnesses today against you, that I have set before you life and death, blessing and cursing; therefore choose life, that both you and your descendants may live."

My friend Linda, who encouraged me to go to our amazing youth group, even bought me a purity ring for my 18th or 19th birthday. Those rings are not cheap. I was very blessed to have her as a friend. I wore that ring every day as a reminder to keep waiting. This symbol helped me when I became weak. It gave me courage and strength. There was someone out there just for me. But, in the meantime, I continued to grow spiritually, learning to rise above my imperfections and become an overcomer.

At home I was withdrawing into myself. My parents were fighting a lot. My family seemed to be falling apart. I took long walks when trying to figure something out, enjoying the scenery and praying. I always took Pugzie and all the neighborhood dogs followed. One time I woke up early and decided to take a walk in one of the surrounding fields. We were walking toward a group of trees when a coyote jumped out at us. All the big dogs ran off like chickens while little Pugzie chased the wild dog away. Size does not matter when love is great. This is not the only time she came to the rescue. I had a cousin staying with me for the weekend while the rest of the family was gone. The first night, Pugzie started running from the sliding glass door at the back porch to the front door, whining. She started to bark. I figured that she really had to use the bathroom. I let her out the front door. She continued to growl and bark. I felt a funny feeling. Something was not right. I opened the front door and stepped out. I heard a male voice quietly trying to entice my dog to come to him. I yelled for Pugzie to come, she didn't listen, and went back inside. Most of the lights were off in the house. I told my cousin that someone was out there and she freaked. She wanted to run into a closet and hide. I ran through the house and turned all the lights on and called Aunt Betty, who was now divorced and living with someone else. Her boyfriend came over right away and walked around the property. When he looked out to the river, some men in a canoe were paddling away. I later learned that some thieves were going up the river stealing what they could. I guess our house was next on the list. Pugzie came back into the house wagging her little tail. She stayed close for the rest of the night. A dog who is loved knows how to truly love back. I sure miss her.

I continued to struggle with who I was meant to be and my desire for a soul mate. I started to think that finding my soul mate would solve all my issues. I would be a wife and eventually a mother and the rest would fall into place. Just like magic. I had a friend who dreamed about a guy and then later met him in public. They both knew they were meant for each other. I wanted this to happen to me so badly that one night I prayed hard to find my soon-to-be-husband. I was pushing for it. I received a quick glimpse of a guy in our youth group. I didn't like this guy in that way. I just wanted to be friends. So, I fought it for a very long time. I loved his family. They were awesome. I was good friends with his sister. But I didn't want him to be the one. During Sunday worship one morning I was singing with my eyes closed giving God my love, when I opened them and saw this guy, Kurt, up on stage playing the guitar. I was hit hard with, "If this is my will, will you follow?" There was dead silence in my head, which is unusual for me. I knew in my heart if this was what God wanted I would follow. I loved Him more than my own desires. I talked to his parents first. With jittery nerves, I walked up to them one Sunday after church service and nervously said, "I think God is calling me to be Kurt's future wife." His mom seemed hopeful. His dad smiled and said, "Could be." We left it at this and decided to see what would come of it. I let it go and decided that if it was meant to be it will happen.

Though I let it go I bonded strongly with his family, the Wicks. I loved his mom Tammy, a tall woman with a continuous smile on her face. I started to call her mom. She was a spiritual mother to me. I learned from her a gentle humbleness and admired the respect she had for her husband. I watched how she mothered her children and the other kids in the youth group. I learned so much from her. She had me stay with her, her daughter, and the youngest boy for a week while the other guys were gone. She had four sons and a daughter, everyone tall and athletic. While I stayed with them my parents sold their house on the river and moved, renting a small house in town. There wasn't much room for me, so my spiritual mom and family let me and Pugzie move in for a time. I believe this was probably strange to her oldest son, Kurt. He was at my parent's house helping with a project and he called my mom, "mom." He didn't know my mom like I did his, and I think he did this out of irritation from me calling his mom, "mom." I wasn't the only one to call her "mom." Many of the other kids in the youth group did too, because she cared for us like another mother.

Finally, when Kurt came up to me to talk about me being his future wife, he told me, "I don't think we are meant to be. I don't feel this way toward you. I just see you as a friend." I totally understood what he meant.

"I think you're right, because that's how I feel about you too," I replied. With a little bit of confusion over the whole ordeal, I completely let it go. It was a very weird situation. All because I had to figure out who my future husband was. (Side note: it might be a good idea not to search for things that are not meant to be just at that point in time, allow life to flow living one day at a time.) Big surprise! It turned out not to be him, of course. I believe God may have been testing me while I worshiped him. I believe there are times in life were God sees if we are willing to put Him before ourselves and trust Him, like with Abraham and Isaac Genesis 22 when God asked Abraham to sacrifice his son and then stopped him right before he was about to kill Isaac.

Abraham was tested. We can and will also be tested. After my experience with Kurt I started to understand that I needed to simplify my beliefs in understanding truth. I needed to get back to the simple basics of truth and rediscover my views. I began to see that un-complicating simple truths by subtracting worldly propaganda such as human thought and emotions made life easier. I saw that I needed to wipe the slate clean, like when I took down the picture collage off my walls. I needed to reevaluate my beliefs. This wasn't easy.

In my struggle of wanting answers, wanting to move forward, and seeking truth about who I was, I often lost focus, hazing in and out. Above all, I wanted love. I learned to give God love but I see now that I didn't receive His love as I should. I didn't have a true understanding of what His love was about. I believe this caused me to still have that void to fill. That God-shaped hole. How can I accept something when I don't fully understand it? I once cried out to God to help me love as He loves. My soul was asking to know love. God had a plan. I had a very long road, a dark road ahead of me before I saw the true light of his love.

8. DEATH OF A LOVED ONE

*"But I do not want you to be ignorant, brethren,
concerning those who have fallen asleep, lest you sorrow as others who have no
hope.
For if we believe that Jesus died and rose again,
even so God will bring with Him those who sleep in Jesus."*

*"For this we say to you by the word of the Lord,
that we who are alive and remain until the coming of the Lord
will by no means precede those who are asleep.
For the Lord Himself will descend from heaven with a shout,
with the voice of an archangel, and with the trumpet of God.
And the dead in Christ will rise first.
Then we who are alive and remain shall be caught up together with them in the
clouds
to meet the Lord in the air.
And thus we shall always be with the Lord."*
~1 Thessalonians 4:13-17 (NKJV)

I continued to live with my spiritual mother Tammy and her family, the Wicks. I still felt lost. Everyone seemed to have a destination but me. A man named Don Tucker put together a play called *Power and the Pit*. This play was about dealing with death and the afterlife and how unbelievers and false Christians go to hell and true believers enter Heaven. This play centered on the condition of the heart. Don and a few adults from the church were interviewing young adults to act and travel.

I was alright with not participating. I could picture myself getting stage fright, freezing on stage, and not being able to move. I would miss everybody, though, since the cast was made up of nearly our entire youth group. But God had different plans for me. A family with two kids I babysat every now and again came to me and said they had some extra funds they didn't know what to do with and felt that God wanted me to have it. I was stunned. At first I said I couldn't take the money. They strongly felt I needed it. Their funds matched exactly the amount required to join *Power and the Pit*. I thought about it for a moment and felt God telling me to accept this gift, so I accepted.

There I was, with this road opening before me that I was supposed to follow. I should have been ecstatic because I now had a direction. All I felt was an amazing sense of peace, until I was waiting at the church to be interviewed. I started to get nervous. I kept telling myself that I knew these people and that God has shown me that this was where he wanted me. They called me in. I wanted to run. I marched into the room and forced myself to smile at the four sets of eyes staring at me.

Mr. Wicks was there, but it didn't help. They gave me a situation where a child was lost and wanted to find his mommy. I was to act it out as I would in real life. I felt ridiculous talking to an imaginary kid. I took hold of my emotions and played out the scene. I tried to pretend that they weren't there. It helped to picture a real child I knew, acting how I would act with this child. I bent down and comfortingly said, "It's alright, what's wrong?" I paused as if the child was talking to me. I schooled my features into a look of concern. I then looked around like I was looking for the mother. I smiled as I looked at the child again and gently said, "I'll help you find your mommy. Take my hand and we'll walk around and call out to her. What's your mommy's name?" I listened and grabbed the child's hand, then proceeded to walk around calling, "Sarah!" until she was found. I must have been alright because they accepted me. I also felt that God already predestined me to be a part of this group.

The Wick family would be going. It felt like a huge family trip. My best friend, Jennie, was going and so was Trevor. We spent many weeks preparing, practicing the play, purchasing costumes and accessories, and learning how to put on stage make-up. The Wick boys were turning two greyhound buses into half-bus, half-bed and bath. The married adults would sleep on the buses while the rest of us (the cast) would either be in a hotel or tent.

The day came to shove off. We said goodbye to family and friends in the parking lot. We were all excited to be a part of something so big.

I now get made fun of for being a part of *Power and the Pit*, but I wouldn't have changed being a part of this play. This experience brought a lot of growth and maturity to me. We went from town to town through a few states in the northwest acting, performing, singing, and spreading the good news of Jesus Christ. Sometimes we stayed with host families.

We met some amazing people. One family I remember well lived in California. I stepped out of the air-conditioned bus into a suburb with hot, humidly stale air. I actually thought about trying to fry an egg on a sidewalk. The glimpse I got as I ran for the house and the cool indoors was of a cute Mexican-style house. The house was beige in color with a small archway and a tiny manicured lawn. The family was friendly and caring. We made popcorn that I spilled all over the kitchen floor and watched *The Prince of Egypt* Disney movie. Two girls and I stayed while the others went to different host families. I loved staying with host families rather than the hotels or camp grounds. As we continued to travel some places were spiritually cold and others were warm with a friendly atmosphere.

Acting wasn't as bad as I thought. I did alright in my slumber party girl's scene. It helped my stage fright to be on stage with a little group. A group of girls decide to go to a fast food place for a late night snack. On the way, we get into a fatal car accident with a car filled with gang members. We stand before the judgment seat. A slumber party girl who is a fake Christian goes to hell while one of the gang members who is starting to turn his life around goes to heaven.

Our group grew tired from traveling, lack of sleep, and the constant packing and unpacking. We began irritating each other. Someone came up with the idea of a 411 session, dialing numbers for information. Since our gathering consisted of giving information on our issues this is what we named it. We would circle up in a group, explain our issues. It could be a problem against each other or just a problem we were facing. Whatever the issue was we all helped to work it out, strengthening our friendships with each other and allowing a lot of growth in our mental and emotional states of being. We learned so much from each other. It also taught me to talk out my problems by going to the source to make things right. There was a lot of love in this group.

We stopped in Denver Colorado for a week. My first thought was of Daren. My life truly seems to run in circles. We were camping this time, and performing at a church where some kids who were killed in the Columbine shooting the year before had attended. I could feel the hurt and grief of this church. There wasn't a large turnout from the church itself, but there was a group of Asians who showed up and accepted a relationship with Jesus.

Daren also showed up. Mom had called and let him know that I was in town. It was nice to see him. I no longer had feelings for him and was no longer controlled by my physical needs of believing I had to have a boyfriend. After the play, he asked if I could go to dinner with him and his friend. I ended up going with my best friend and another friend from school who was a part of our youth group.

After dinner, we hung out in the parking lot of the church with everyone else. At the end of the night I hugged Daren goodbye. He gave me his number. Once we got to camp we all turned in. Traveling and the hard work of putting the stage up and then tearing it down were taking its toll, although I got to skip chores that night. Soon, all too soon, morning came. We were planning a barbeque that day. Things were quiet and relaxed. The day felt peaceful.

At noon, Bella came up to me with a phone she borrowed. She said, "That friend of yours seems nice. You should call him and invite him to the barbeque." I refused at first but she kept bugging and bugging. I started to think she might be interested in him. I was uneasy about using a phone that didn't belong to either one of us. But she wouldn't give up.

I called Daren. I barely said, "Hello!" before he blurted out, "I was just about to get in my car and come find you. You saved me a trip. Your mom called me and your brother is in the hospital with some fatal injuries." My brain couldn't process this.

"What?" I asked.

He repeated, "Your brother, Levi was in a car accident. His injuries are fatal." I stared dumbfounded at nothing, looking off into space. Shoving the phone at Bella, I burst into tears and ran to the tent I was sharing with some other girls. I sat on my sleeping bag shaking uncontrollably. I couldn't breathe. I felt sick. Bella must have talked to Daren because soon everyone was surrounding me. I remember feeling that I wanted to be left alone. I didn't know what to do. I couldn't think. They got ahold of my mom, then handed me the phone. She wanted me there. I couldn't think straight, I needed help.

Don Tucker purchased a flight back to Spokane. Bella was going with me. She had to leave for a wedding in a few days as it was. We rushed, packing what was necessary, and within a few hours it was time to go. Everyone stood in a line outside. I felt like a freak show.

On the freeway as we were passing the campground we saw a rainbow covering just the area we were camping in. I was in awe. I knew God was showing me that He was with me, with all of us. He was giving His love and comfort.

Don called Mr. Wicks. "Do you see the rainbow!" He paused to listen, "Yeah! We see it too! What a miracle. God is good." It was very amazing, not a normal day miracle. I seem to be blessed with extraordinary happenings, good and bad.

Bella guided me through the airport. I tried to focus on what we were doing but my brain would not cooperate. We made it onto the plane. I don't remember much of that flight. Bella asked me if I was alright once in a while. I was so glad she came to help me. I thought of my little brother, how I was a part of his pregnancy and birth, how I loved him from the very beginning, and how I became distant from him and the rest of my family in the last few years. I still loved them all deeply.

Bella's mom picked us up from the Spokane airport and drove us straight to the Deaconess Hospital where my brother was in the intensive care unit. I was a bundle of nerves.

We walked through some doors in the hospital and came upon a group of people from our church. There had to be about 20 people there. My family and I hugged. Tears started rolling again. The heart was deep.

It was nice to have so many supporting friends around but I can't say it was comforting. Nothing could comfort this pain.

They told me what happened. Levi was camping with his best friend and family. He and his best friend went to hunter safety class. The older brother, who had just started driving, picked them up in a small pickup. On their way back to camp, he drove right past a stop sign into an intersection. A woman driving a diesel truck plowed right into them knocking the little pickup senseless. The kids and pickup flew and flipped over and over. My brother was in the middle. Levi's best friend died at the scene and the other boy, along with Levi, was in critical condition. I heard later from somewhere that the woman who was driving had to seek emotional therapy in response to their deaths. It's difficult to understand how one act can affect so many people.

We were all waiting for answers and hoping for a miracle. The waiting was torture. I was sick to my stomach. I didn't want to eat though someone tried to make me. The food was like eating cardboard, and I couldn't get it past the lump in my throat. I tried to rest but the pain was too much. Dad and Mom prayed for a miracle. I did not want my brother to die. I wanted him on earth, with us. We had the sad news that the older boy passed on. Soon the news came that Levi was brain-dead. If by chance he continued to live, he would be a vegetable for the rest of his life. My dad made the decision to pull the plug. We all agreed. It was better knowing he was in heaven with a full life rather than here on earth not really existing. We all went to his room where he was on life support.

We all said our goodbyes. I walked up to him and held his cold, clammy hand. I looked upon his bruised face. He didn't even look like the boy I knew. His head was swollen to the size of a watermelon. It was so hard to let go. I whispered, "Goodbye, I love you." I walked back to the rest of the group. We all stood in a semicircle before him, all in tears, and all hurting so deep. The doctor removed life support. There was the sound of silence that echoed into our souls. All three boys were gone from our world of hardships, pain, and sorrow, never to share another smile with us. The boy I once knew who used to run around slapping at mosquitoes and playing with Lego's and hot wheels was gone. I used to pretend to be a horse for him, even tying a bedroll to my back so he could pretend to be a cowboy. He also loved to go fishing. I felt guilty for not being close to him the last couple of years. I will always love him completely within my heart.

I don't know how we made it home to Newdock. But we were there, where my parents now lived on Scotti RD on the outskirts of town. We awaited his funeral. People brought tons of food, but I still could not eat. I was completely sick to the stomach with heart-wrenching pain. The days were long, the nights torture. It was almost like a punishment to live while my brother was dead. I prayed a lot and leaned on God through this time. People usually want to blame God, but I knew this was not of Him. The Bible says that all good gifts come from God. Anything else comes from the dark one. Even though I knew Levi asked Jesus into his heart and that he was in heaven, it still hurt. Although the pain excruciating, I have now realized that it was still far from darkness. The pain I felt was from the deep love I had for him. There is no darkness in love. Everything I went through was an emotional process of grief. Real love continues to love when it hurts.

The day of the funeral arrived. There were so many people. It felt like the whole town showed up. There was so much love and support from everyone. The sanctuary doors had to be open because there weren't enough seats or standing space. This is a day I will never forget. There were large pictures of Levi on each side of his coffin. I could hear crying. Pastor Kenneth's eulogy was personal and gentle since he knew our family. A slideshow played accompanied by the song, "I will remember you" by Sarah McLachlan. There were a lot of sighs and laughter. My favorite was the picture of Levi in the fridge drinking out of the milk carton. He had to be about five or six years old. I didn't want it to end. I just wanted to sit there and watch and listen forever.

All too soon it was time to head to the cemetery where he was to be buried next to his best friend. A huge bouquet of roses was placed on his coffin. Family members were encouraged to take one. I carefully took one, planning to keep it forever. Then the coffin was lowered down into the ground. It gave me the sense of finality, that it was all coming to a close. A part of me didn't want it to end while another part was telling me it was time to keep on living. Once everything was accomplished and we all said another goodbye it was time to head home. I turned to leave and right before me stood this young girl. She asked if she could have my rose. I looked at her. At first I was shocked that someone would ask such a thing and then remembered that Levi had a girl he was sweet on. She wasn't allowed to date so Levi promised to wait for her. I knew this had to be her. I had so much to remember Levi by but she didn't. I gave her my rose. She thanked me and I could see the relief fill her face. She was probably so scared to ask while at the same time greatly desiring to have one of Levi's roses. I still don't regret giving it to her, and I never will. It did my heart good to help someone else. It was very strange to feel good about one thing while suffering about another. But that is love.

My family was no longer the same. We were missing a member, but life had to continue. I went to the wedding Bella was in, a week later, at the same church. Linda Morell was getting married, the same girl I had always been jealous of. It was good to see the good in life continue.

The wedding was a nice distraction, but after it was done Bella would be flying back to join *Power and the Pit*. I was given the choice to stay or join back up with them. I chose the latter. I needed to be active. I needed to get back to life. I was sad but I was alright. Bella and I left to join back up with our group. It felt good to see their faces, although I didn't like being treated like porcelain. I wanted things to go back to normal, as normal as they could get. A few things were hard to deal with. We were in Oregon, where I was from, and where most of my relatives lived. We went to Newdock Beach. If you know this area of Oregon, you know the roads to the coast are extremely curvy and dangerous in bad conditions. It was a nice day, but we were all in those greyhound size buses. These buses took up quite a bit of the road. One day, a young man in a little pickup wanted to go faster than us. He passed both of our buses and sped away. We came around the corner and right onto the aftermath of that same little pickup's head on collusion with a family in a minivan.

Don and Mr. Wick pulled the buses to the side of the road and called 911. A couple of young adults from the cast with emergency training jumped off the bus to help. I stayed in the bus at first. But I had to see. I left the bus and took a deep breath while I looked. I felt numb at first. A few friends asked if I was alright. I just nodded. There wasn't much I could do so I prayed. The minivan had two parents and three kids. The people helping out from our group stayed calm, talked to the victims, and helped in any way they could until the ambulance showed. From what I remember the children were the only ones who survived. I thought deeply on the word death, a word most of us dread. Death, I see now, is not something to be feared. It is a part of life. It is a doorway from this world into the next. Yes, it can be very painful, but both the ones left behind and the victims of death's call still continue to live in memories, in hearts, and in the spiritual world. Death is not truly death unless it's the blackness of one's soul, and the unbelief in Jesus and His light of love and life.

As I was trying to deal with all my chaotic emotions created by all this death around me, I was trying to find the good, wanting purpose to come from it all. My brother's death became a part of the message at the end of our show. I was asked if I wanted to come and share since I had family members in the audience. I wasn't sure if I wanted to experience stage fright in that moment. But when it came time to share I decided to. I botched it. I so wanted good to result from Levi's death that I mumbled and jumbled about how it was bringing my family closer together, something I truly wanted to believe. In reality, my parent's marriage had fallen apart. It had been struggling for some time.

While I was struggling with all this I had a woman come up to me and say, "I feel that I need to tell you that God has an eagle for your future husband, and that someone is going to come into your life for a while filled with hot air. Do not listen to this person." Filled with hot air means to lash out with anger and hate. It was nice to hear something about my future husband and I acknowledged the warning about the other. There was definitely highs and lows during this time.

Levi is not dead. He lives. He is more alive than I am. I live in a figure that holds my soul at a crossroad of life and death, a temple that I fight to fill with light and love, but which can become consumed with darkness and pain. Levi now lives without struggles. He also lives in memories, in hearts, and he lives in heaven, where our home really is and no death can reach him. I live each day knowing that I haven't seen the last of him. Someday, when I'm called home, I will see his cute smiling face again. God is not being cruel when taking loved ones home. He does not see death as we do. Death to Him is us being rebirthed into everlasting life, if we follow the path of truth and righteousness. The death we need to fight against is spiritual death.

9. RUNNING FROM HARDSHIPS

"You therefore must endure hardship as a good soldier of Jesus Christ."
~ 2 Timothy 2:3

I tried to move forward in Christ after Levi's death, but it was hard. My wounds were still tender. I didn't want to endure the hardships of life. My life seemed to become one struggle after the other. Through everything, I did my best to love and do the right thing, but I struggled deep down with sorrow and pain.

My traveling and acting days were soon over. Our journey of *Power and the Pit* was finished. We were back at home. I went back to work at Safeway. I was still living with the Wicks. Daniel came to me and asked if I would start paying 20 dollars a week for living there, the same amount they were asking of Kurt. I felt like one of their kids with both Daniel and Tammy teaching me life lessons right along with their kids. I was humbled. I loved them for it. I had no problem giving them 20 dollars a week. But, I moved out by the end of that week.

The reason I moved was because Jennie, my best friend, moved in with the Crollins. They had an extra room and she wanted me to move in too. We both thought this would be a great idea. I approached Kelly Crollins, who said she would love for me to move in.

So, it was settled. Pastor Craig agreed to keep Pugzie for a while. He was an animal lover, though he did complain when Pugzie peed on his carpet. This is something she did when she wanted to show she wasn't happy about something. I don't think she was happy about being without me.

Although I was growing spiritually, I was still missing something. I continued to believe it to be my soulmate. I was always on the lookout. This time of my life seemed to pass much too slowly. I wanted to fast-forward to the time I would meet Mr. Right. But in the meantime, I had my friends and family. I was constantly doing things, looking for fun times, and going wherever I wanted to. This was the best time of my life though somewhat dampened after all the pain I experienced. I lived, I was free, and I loved with the love I knew.

Not long after I moved in with the Crollins, my dad contacted me and told me that Granny Eileen was dying of cancer. She'd smoked two packs of cigarettes each day for life. Now she struggled from the cancer in her lungs. She was also an alcoholic. She would put a lid on her glass in the mornings with a straw to hide the fact that she was drinking hard alcohol, but we all knew. She was my favorite grandma though. I always felt close to her. Granny Eileen and I were always excited to see each other whenever the family visited her. I would play tricks on her such as turning over the plastic mat she had by the front door so that the poky underside was exposed. Granny would walk out barefooted, we'd flip the plastic mat over, and she would dance with ouches and screeches when she came back in. My siblings and I would giggle with glee. Then she would smile and say, "You guys got me again!" She usually found a way to get me back. She also spoiled me with the best treats like going to Dairy Queen, letting me get into her candy stash, and spending time taking me for a drive to the city park.

As my dad was telling me about her cancer, I started to struggle with more pain. I wasn't sure how to react to another death in the family. It was a fresh layer of sad emotion on someone who was already hurting. Each day there were moments where I literally felt like I was drowning. Dad also told me that Granny Eileen wanted me to stay with her and help her out. I would be taking her to her doctor appointments and helping her with her medication. I told my dad I would do it. I was moving to Oregon for who knew how long. I packed everything I thought I would need. I left my unreliable car, a blue Ford Tempo, since it broke down all the time. Dad drove me to Grandmother's house. In the back of my mind I thought maybe Mr. Right could be in Oregon. I was tired of waiting. I wanted my life to change for the better. I thought a man would complete me and that marriage was the answer to everything, a fix for all my troubles.

I quit my job and had to find a permanent home for Pugzie. My life became too unstable to keep her. She needed stability. No one I knew wanted a dog so I decided to take her to the local pet shop and see if they could find her a home. I refused to take her to the pound. The owner of the store agreed. I told him that I would be back to see if she was still there. If she was I would take her back and figure something else out. I bought a leash for her and we tied her to the checkout stand. My heart broke as I walked away from her. She whimpered as I left the store. Deep down I was hoping she would still be there at the end of the day. But I knew that it wouldn't be practical. Why does life have to be so hard? When I came back that evening she was gone.

I never felt so disappointed in my life. I went to my car and cried, praying that someday I would see her again just to know she was alright.

At Granny's house, I moved into dad's old bedroom. Granny and I drove around and looked at the town sights. We even went to the park just to see the activity going on like old times. I got a library card so I could check out books to read in my spare time. I remember reading 12 books in just over a week. I loved my Granny Eileen and was happy to help, but I was often not really needed.

One day, Granny decided to visit a friend and find an orchard to pick some apples. I woke up with a huge migraine. It was making me sick. She said she had some aspirin and handed me a pill. It looked like an aspirin. With heavy, watery eyes, I took the aspirin and we got ready to go, heading out in her silver Thunderbird. Everything seemed fine. I was enjoying the greenness of Oregon. My head dropped. I woke back up instantly and looked at Granny. I told her I was feeling very tired. My head kept bobbing up and down as I fought to stay awake. I looked at Granny again and asked her, "What kind of pill did you give me?" She just shrugged her shoulders. We stopped at her friend's house. I slept with my head in my arms on the kitchen table.

We left her friend's and headed to an orchard. I was once again bobbing my head up and down. I just wanted to head back to the house where I could sleep off the rest of whatever she gave me. Granny pulled to the side of the road by some apple trees. We got out, Granny grabbed a box from the trunk, and we picked some apples. I figured we would pick the apples and then go to the farm and pay for them. Our family would do this a lot when we came to visit. When Granny decided she had enough apples, we got back into the car and Granny drove away. I realized that Granny Eileen was stealing apples! I said, "Granny we have to pay for those!" she shushed me. I was seeing a whole new side to my grandma. Maybe she drugged me on purpose? When we returned home, I laid on the couch and slept for hours.

Granny started to have doctor appointments almost weekly. Her cancer was progressing. She wasn't allowed to drive anymore because of the medication she was on. She wanted to find a church to go to. I was excited about this! I had prayed for her for a long time to find God. She had a lot of hurt and anger from her past. We tried a couple of different churches in the area but they all seemed cold. There was no one to encourage us or help us feel welcome; it was so different from what I was used to.

Granny lost interest. I was also disappointed. I really wanted to find a connection somewhere. Paul writes in Romans 14: 13 that believers should not "put a stumbling block or a cause to fall in our brother's way." There is nothing worse than a cold church. A cold church will cause stumbling blocks and create a cause to fall. The church may not realize how off-putting it could be. Churches should open their arms to newcomers as the angels rejoice for each saved soul. Smiling faces and a warm greeting do wonders. They encourage people to continue coming by drawing them in. But sadly, Granny Eileen eventually lost interest in finding a church.

Since I was the driver, Granny decided to buy me a car. I found a cranberry colored Dodge Neon that was a rental car and didn't have too many miles on it. She paid for the car in full. It felt good to be able to drive my own car around. She said it was payment for coming to help her. I soon found out that she thought she had control of me just because she bought me something. When she did things, it came with strings. The car gave me more autonomy, but Granny fought for control over everything I did. When she didn't need me, I visited other family on my mom's side. It was refreshing not to be so bored all the time.

Having known Granny since I was a little girl, I began to notice a change in her personality. I was asked by our next door neighbors, a nice Christian family, to watch their chubby, adopted, one-year- old baby girl. I had nothing better to do. Granny was always cooing over this little kid. I figured I could take care of the baby and keep an eye on Granny. I thought the baby would cheer her up.

Granny had a fit. I had never seen her react this way so I stayed at the neighbor's house with the child. When the parents returned, I told them about Granny's reaction and that I wouldn't be able to babysit again. They understood, and even became a haven when I needed to talk to someone about Granny. Galatians 6:1 tells us, "Brethren, if a man is overtaken in any trespass, you who are spiritual restore such a one in a spirit of gentleness." The neighbors definitely loved. They helped me through this burden with gentleness. I may not have found a church but I had loving Christian neighbors.

I started spending more time with Aunt Jan. I have to give Aunt Jan credit because she was always there for Granny. She chose to live close and be a part of Granny's life when Granny treated her badly from past grudges long before I was born. I think Aunt Jan felt that I was moving into her territory sometimes because Granny wouldn't give her any appreciation for the things she helped out with while Granny fawned over me. But I was fast falling out of grace in Granny's eyes.

After I had lived with Granny for several months, she had surgery to get a tracheal tube. She would be at the hospital for a week. My cousin Jenny would be here that same week. She wanted to stay with me. I told Granny about it, that I would be doing things with Jenny when I wasn't at the hospital. She seemed fine with it. I enjoyed my time with my cousin. It was nearing the end of the week and we decided to go spend some time with her dad who lived in Newdock Beach. I brought Granny home on Friday. Aunt Jan was going to help her while I was gone for one night that weekend. Everything seemed fine. I see now that I was very naive and a bit self-centered. As I think about it now she must have been going through so many fears and negative emotions. I should have stayed to help Granny with her new condition. I was used to being independent and on my own, and I was running from the difficulty and pain of Granny's circumstances.

The curvy road on the way to the beach reminded me of the crash with the family in the minivan. Jenny and I arrived safely. Uncle Bill's house was on the beach and we spent a lot of time walking the dogs. We ate at his girlfriend's restaurant for free. We cruised around the popular boardwalk area and checked out guys. Uncle Bill was always fun. He liked to joke and would plan fun activities. He took us on a little white water rafting trip where we were soaked to the skin. All too soon, our visit came quickly to an end. We were getting ready to head back to Granny's when it started to down pour. It was raining so hard that you couldn't see very far ahead of you. I kept picturing that little pickup that was driving raucously on the curvy narrow road, and then crashing into the minivan. I called Aunt Jan telling her my situation. She said she would check in on Granny. I then called Granny. She couldn't talk, so I just told her, "I'm stuck due to the weather. Aunt Jan will check in on you and I will be on my way back as soon as the rain lets up." It rained for a long time. We ended up staying another night. I worried about Granny the whole time.

When I got back to Granny's, she would not talk to me. I didn't know what to do about her moodiness. I had never seen this side of her before. I figured it might be the medication they had her on. In reality, there probably were many factors in her mood swings, including fear of death, and unhappiness about her situation. I wish I would have been more sensitive to her needs, but I didn't understand much about them at this time of my young life. This was all a difficult lesson to learn.

It all came to a breaking point. Granny was going crazy. She wanted me out. This was very frustrating to her because she had to motion with her hands and form words with her mouth. She had no voice. She was becoming very hard-hearted. She wanted the title to my car. I went looking for it. She opened the door and started digging. I told her I would find it. I was so angry at her. I wanted to find it and hand it to her to show her I didn't care if she took back the car. But it was nowhere. She thought I was keeping it from her. She motioned down a police car. The officer stopped and came over. Granny was very hysterical. You'd think I was a burglar. I apologized to him. I explained the situation while Granny was looking for something to write with. I let them communicate. He walked over to me and told me that there wasn't much he could do about this situation, that if I needed anything to call for help. This made Granny really angry. She told me to take the car and leave.

I walked over to the neighbors to get a breather. This whole situation shook me. I went from being Granny's helper to her disappointment. I didn't know what to do. She wanted me gone so I figured I would go back home, where I was wanted, back to family and friends. So, I packed up my stuff and left. I ran away. I blasted my music all the way back to Newdock. It felt good to be home. But a week later my dad got a phone call from Aunt Jan. Granny had to be rushed to the hospital. She took a fall down her basement stairs and wasn't going to survive. Dad wanted me to go.

"She doesn't want to see me," I told him. "I let her down!"

"You need to go anyways," Dad said.

The drive was long and quiet. When we pulled up to the house and went in, Aunt Jan was waiting for us to help clean up the mess in the kitchen. There was blood all over the sink. After Granny fell down the stairs she struggled back up to the kitchen and coughed up a huge chunk of fleshy meat. I wondered if it was part of a lung. I was weighed down with guilt.

"I should have been here. I should have stuck it out and not run from this problem." I decided right then and there that I would stick out the hardships from now on. Romans 5:3-4 says, "We also glory in tribulations, knowing tribulations produces perseverance; and perseverance, character; and character, hope. Now hope does not disappoint, because the love of God has been poured out in our hearts by the Holy Spirit who was given to us." I did not love when I ran from hardships and tribulations.

After all the cleaning was done we went to the hospital. I sat in a chair next to Granny's room. Dad pushed me in to see her. She turned her head from me and pretended to be sleeping when I walked in. I wanted to say I was sorry, and that I love her, but the words wouldn't come. I was so ashamed of not staying. I felt like this was my entire fault. I figured the best thing I could do was let her die in peace without me there. Getting to know Granny for the last three months showed me how stubborn she was. I wasn't going to be able to get through to her. So, I sat in the hall and prayed. A preacher came to console her. I prayed that she would be sincere when she said her prayer for salvation.

I lived with the guilt of running from this hardship for years. I would constantly pray for forgiveness and for my Granny's soul. It took me years to realize that I didn't feel forgiveness because I wasn't forgiving myself. I was the one who kept this wound open and bleeding. Once I forgave myself for running and not sticking it out the wound healed and I was able to move forward in that area of my life. I realized in not forgiving myself that I hated myself.

When I was finally home to stay, things went back to normal for the most part. I was so happy to be back at church. I'd missed my church family. They brought me out of my depressions. But I found myself jumping from one hard situation into another. My youth pastor Craig received a phone call from a paraplegic. A man who had broken his neck a few years ago needed someone to come Fridays and Saturdays so his caregiver could have those days off. Pastor Craig approached me about it. He thought I would be perfect for the job.

My first day on the job the caregiver walked me through everything—how to change a catheter, etc. As I got to know Dick, I could see that he was a nice enough fellow, and I enjoyed our conversations. After my second weekend on the job I got a phone call from one of the caregiver's daughters. She explained that her mom ran off and has been gone for a few days. The girls, who were in their early teens, were there alone with Dick. They needed me to come and help. I went over right away.

The caregiver never came back. I ended up having to move in and become the permanent caregiver. The youngest girl moved in with a family member, but the oldest girl was almost 14 and stayed for a while. I thought it was kind of strange. But she eventually moved in with a friend. I found this situation to be completely weird. The Human Resource manager was coming and going, and she walked me through the process of becoming a licensed caregiver. I was not sure where this road was headed or if I wanted to walk this journey. But this man needed someone now.

I learned more about the situation he was living in. He had suffered abuse and neglect by his caregiver. I was appalled by some of his stories. I really wanted to help this guy out, so after all the paper work was done, I started to organize and clean his single wide trailer. I took the back bedroom for myself. My dad installed a buzzer in my room where Dick could push a button if he had an emergency. The first night, after I feel asleep, he buzzed me. I rushed out and asked him what was wrong. He just smiled and said that he just wanted to see if it would work. He thought he was so funny. I began to hate that buzzer. It went off almost all night long. Dick would fall asleep with it in his hand, and in his sleep, he would continually push the buzzer. I would panic and come running out. I soon started to take the buzzer out of his hand after the first buzz.

There was a retired RN next door who we hired to come and bathe Dick. That was not something I was comfortable with. Thanksgiving came around and we had an awesome dinner. Dick was an amazing cook. He couldn't actually cook anymore so he told me what to do. That was the best Thanksgiving dinner since great Granny Agnes's holiday meals. Dad and Mom even said so. When Christmas came around we cut a tree and put it up. Dick loved to play chess so I picked up a stone chess set. I had fun decorating all by myself. When Christmas day came, we opened presents. He loved his chess set, and I loved the paint set he got me. He said it was the best Christmas he had in a long time.

But soon after the holidays when I was cleaning some cupboards, I came across a Bong. Dick said it belonged to the caregiver before me. I was going to toss it. He argued that it wasn't right because it didn't belong to us. He was getting so worked up about it that I gave in for the time being. I figured I would wait a couple days then get rid of it. The other caregiver was never going to come back. I had no use for it.

That night he asked that I keep the door unlocked, he had a friend coming over to watch TV with him. A guy next door who was H.I.V positive would often come and visit Dick. He seemed like a nice guy. I didn't know him well, so I was uncomfortable about it. But I figured I could lock my bedroom door. That night, when they thought I was asleep, I could smell pot. I realized that my situation could get dangerous. I let this go on for a couple of nights while I tried to figure out what to do. There was a fitness place in town hiring for their daycare. I applied for the position.

I next confronted Dick about the pot. He tried to deny it. Then he said he needed it for the seizures. I understood but he didn't have a prescription. I also learned that the 14-year-old that stayed for a while helped him smoke the stuff while I was transitioning into the position of his caregiver. She'd hid the pipe.

Dick realized that I wasn't going to stick around. He wouldn't look me in the eye anymore. A couple he was friends with were visiting. I took the opportunity to go grocery shopping. When I came back Dick informed me that they were going to start caring for him. I was fine with this. I was worried about finding another caregiver. I didn't want Dick to be in another bad situation.

Forms were signed and things were going smoothly. The wife needed a ride to a friend's to pick some stuff up. I gave her a ride. While I was parked outside waiting for her to get what she needed I heard a familiar bark. It couldn't be! I got out of my car and sure enough there was Pugzie. I cried. She ran into my arms. I smothered her with love and kisses. She did the same. Her new owner came out. I told her who I was. She said I could come back anytime to see her. As I drove away I knew I wouldn't be back. It was a bitter sweet moment. I was happy to know she had a good home but sad to have to leave her again. It was best to stay away. I was thankful to God for answering my prayer.

10. MEETING MR. RIGHT

*"So then, they are no longer two but one flesh.
Therefore what God has joined together, let not man separate."*
~Matthew 19:6 (NKJV)

    I know the frustration of pining away for a perfect man. I also now know after finding Mr. Right that dating is completely different than marriage. When dating, we look for every chance to be together. We go out to dinner, movies, and just hang out together enjoying each other's company. Everything goes smoothly. Both sides of the family are friendly and trying to show the best of themselves. This is how it started out for me. My life was changing. The course I found myself on was leading me into the arms of my future husband.

    Grandma Whitaker, who now lived in Newdock, wanted me to start taking care of Grandpa as his part-time caregiver. My cousin Joshua took over for the other part-time. I kept jumping from one caregiving position to another when it wasn't something I really wanted to do. I wasn't sure what I wanted to do, but this door was opened to me. In Exodus, God opens the door for baby Moses to enter into the royal family, and when Moses is a grown man, God closes the door on this life. God had a bigger plan for Moses. Maybe God opened that door to answer my prayer to know that Pugzie was happy and healthy. Maybe I was a prayer answered for Dick who needed someone while struggling at his own crossroad. When it was time for that door to close, he opened another to help me get out of that situation. I also got the daycare job at the fitness center which was on the days I didn't have to be at my grandparents'. Everything was working out nicely. I didn't have much time to be involved with youth group and family while I was taking care of Dick. It felt so good to have more freedom. I loved being around the family, including my church family, again.

One day, I walked to Mom's house, who was now living just down the road from Grandma after her and Dad's separation. She had some mail for me from one of her older sisters, my Aunt Marge. She mailed me the title to my car. Somehow, when I visited her in Oregon, it ended up on her floor. I looked at Mom and asked, "How in the world did that happen?" I was very relieved to have the title, but it made me sad. I wish things were different with Granny Eileen in the end. The guilt I held crept up on me. That guilt was hard to live with. I would start praying for forgiveness every time I felt it attacking me. In this time of my life I didn't know why it kept attacking. I didn't understand that it was because I wasn't forgiving myself.

I was very stubborn in my religion. I was seeking and just figuring out a relationship with Christ. I may have been raised in the church but finding a relationship with Jesus didn't start until the day I chose to live for Him. I was a toddler in this relationship. My grandmother would have the Mormons and Jehovah's Witnesses come in to sit and visit her. I would hide in my room. I told Grandma I didn't believe the way they did. I didn't want to be a part of the visit. This made Grandma mad. I was like a child with little understanding wanting to shy away from the things that would confuse me. Grandma told me that I was being rude, and she was right, I was.

As the same two young Mormon men would come for a visit with their clean short haircuts and Mormon bibles at their side, Grandma seeped with gaiety for the company, except when she would lecture me, "You need to visit with them too! There is nothing wrong with a visit." I would stubbornly reply, in the famous Whitaker way, "I don't believe the way they do and I don't agree with them!" Grandma would huff and grumble under her breath. I stuck my nose in the air as I shut myself up in my room next to the kitchen. I would listen through the door as she let them in. She was always polite. Then I heard, "I'm sorry about my granddaughter! I just don't know how to get her to join us." I groaned.

I spent the time reading as I waited for them to leave. I thought I was doing what was right. Now I enjoy conversing with people of different beliefs, especially the Jehovah Witnesses. I have met some amazing people with openness and love. Love is a language that all can understand, transcending religion, race, and nationality. But, so is hate. For every positive, there is a negative. It's our choice to choose which one we want to portray. Deuteronomy 30:19 shows us this, "I call heaven and earth as witnesses today against you, that I have set before your life and death, blessing and cursing; therefore choose life, that both you and your descendants may live." God has set before us the consequences of our choices. We are the ones that make the choices of life or death, love or hate.

As I continued to find who I was, who I was meant to be, and discovered true love I thought of a place in Spokane called the prayer room. When I was

20, 16 years ago, a good friend and I visited this place for prayer. I filled out a form concerning what I needed prayer over. It was almost like going to an actual doctor's office. But in this case, it was a place of healing over the soul. I was seeking whatever word God had for me. I was feeling restless in my soul.

As they called me in, just like at a doctor's office, I was a bit nervous. The person praying for me asked if there was anything specific I needed prayer over. I told him that I just wanted whatever word God gave. So, he prayed and then he was silent for a moment. He asked, "Do you write?" I said, "Yes, I have written some short stories and poems." He asked, "Do you have some available for me to see?" I replied, "I have some in my car." I kept them close at hand when I needed to add to my collection. My friend fetched them and the man took a moment to read them. I felt like I was being interviewed for a job or career. He picked the ones he liked the most and said that writing would be a part of my future.

After my visit to the prayer room I went back to my jobs and life. I kept writing here and there when I had a chance, but life soon took over. I found less time to write. I also found myself moving once again. I moved to the upstairs of my mom's house. My parents' divorce was final. I continued to care for my grandpa and work at the fitness center. I spent my free time with my friends, going from one place to another. I was also hanging with my old friend Blair. She was having issues of her own, choosing to leave her husband. As I was helping her, I became friends with Ben, the younger brother of Blair's ex-boyfriend Mick, a guy she'd dated just after high school. When Blair lived with us my senior year, Ben was a senior too, but I thought he was a freshman because of his looks. Ben was interested in me then but I thought he was way too young and a bit of a dork. Now, he'd changed so much I didn't recognize him. He hadn't hit his growth spurt until after he graduated high school and he was now very tall. He was very good looking with his short dark wavy hair and hazel, what my Aunt Paula would call bedroom eyes. His eyes had the romantic sleepy look. We started to hang out quite often. I started to figure out that he liked me a lot. I was amazed that this was the same person. I started to have feelings for him too but was a little unsure if this was the right direction for me.

As we hung out more and more over three weeks, my walls crumbled. When I had friends over to watch movies, he made sure none of my guy friends had the chance to sit by me. He would quickly sit down before anyone else could. But what really got me was finding him shoveling the snow off my doorsteps one night. This showed me he truly cared. I fell for him completely. I cooed and cawed over his thoughtfulness while he stood there with a smile on his face. I found out later that he shoveled them off because he slipped and fell.

We started to talk about our beliefs. I had to make sure we were equally yoked, that we were on the same page, believing in Jesus. Thankfully, we had the same beliefs. I also found out his favorite animal was an eagle. This made me recollect the time that I received the words, "God has an eagle for your future husband." Was this one for me? Everything seemed to fit. We started dating.

It all happened one night while we were sitting on the couch watching a movie, just hanging out. Our hands found themselves inching toward each other. I thought, "Would he just grab my hand already!" Finally, our hands touched, and we held hands. Tingles rushed up my arm. I decided at that moment to jump in with both feet. My whole soul and body sighed with the finality of finding the one for me, the one that was meant to be. He said that he'd prayed for me to be his wife all those years ago when Blair was dating his older brother.

We quickly fell in love. It was hard to separate us. We went out to movies and dinner. I loved sitting next to him and being his special someone. I started to think about the future with him. How we would live, go to church together, and what our kids' names would be. It didn't hit me yet that there would be two of us making these choices.

I started to hang out a lot with his family at the family's mechanic shop in town, mainly because that's where Ben was working. He worked for his dad, a Vietnam vet with a face like a bulldog and red hair going white. I really liked being around Ben's family. His dad was always happy to see me. He had a lot of amusing stories to tell, including one where I pushed my sister out of my dad's truck window when I was little. I remembered pushing her out the window but not going to the mechanic shop with my dad. His mom liked to tease, his younger sister was quiet and polite, and the youngest brother lived in his own world. They all seemed close, with a good family atmosphere. He had two older siblings, another brother (my friend Blair's ex-boyfriend, Mick), and a sister, who I hadn't met yet. They no longer lived at home.

Ben was a middle child, with middle child issues, which I didn't understand then, but do now. The middle child often grows up learning to act out to get attention. One way is doing what will please their parents in order to find a connection because they are often overlooked growing up. They feel left out a lot. This very human and normal behavior was Ben. I, being the oldest of my siblings, had and sometimes still have the oldest child issues. I tend to do things my way, I'm not easily bullied into things, and I often take a stand against things that I feel are not right. These two issues affected both of us soon after we began our journey together.

We had been dating for two months when I overheard a family friend tell someone that they were picking up an engagement ring for Ben. I tried not to give it away that I heard, but they assumed I did. I tried my best to play dumb to what was going on. Ben was going to wait until Christmas to ask, and then decided not to. I was sitting at their kitchen table when he came over and kneeled before me. I instantly knew what was going on but didn't want to ruin the surprise. I tried to act oblivious. I was eager to see the ring and nervous even though I knew what was going on, and I was not sure how to react. When he opened the box, I was very still. The ring was petite and beautiful, a tiny diamond set up on a pedestal with more tiny diamonds running down the silver band on each side of the raised one. I was not into big showy jewels. I loved it. He asked the question, "Will you be my wife?" I whispered, "Yes."

I pretty much moved in with him and his family after that. I continued to work for Grandma but decided to quit working at the fitness center. I still stayed involved with the youth group, but had less time for friends. Also, it does shame me to admit that we became sexually involved before our wedding. He asked me, "Are you a virgin?" I no longer had my flower, that barrier that shows your virginity. But, since I never went all the way, I said, "Yes." I believed, in my mind, I was because I never allowed things to get that far. But, since I no longer had my flower, I actually wasn't. I now understand that even extreme making out is a form of sex. This affected our relationship after we said our vows.

Comparing who Ben was then and who he is now, I see that I have married a strong man. No matter which way the wind would toss us he always made the choice that brought healing and good to our lives. My love for him now is a lot stronger than when we married. We decided to get married in Reno in the month of January. His parents were going there for a big Jeepers meeting. Every year there are gatherings all over in different states where people go jeeping in the mountains. My father-in-law is a coordinator and the head of the one in our area. This made for the perfect opportunity since I had never been much for being the center of attention, especially for a big crowd.

Having a small wedding in Reno was perfectly fine with me. We would have a reception with our friends when we came back. So, in January, we flew to Reno with my mom, sister, and her boyfriend. My dad was coming from Oregon with my younger brother Jason. I was so excited. We were married the first night there. I put on my wedding dress, and Mom put my veil on backwards. I was furious when I saw the pictures, but now I laugh at it. My soon-to-be father-in-law bought me a nice bouquet of flowers. My dad walked me down the aisle of the Holden chapel. The female judge guided us through the process of our vows to each other before God. We kissed. Aside from my sister breaking the news that she was pregnant, everything seemed to be perfect.

Afterward we went to an all-you-can-eat buffet. Afterward my side of the family went their way. My in-laws, hubby, and I explored Reno. I had never been to a place like this, so many bright colorful lights, so many different types of people, and a festive atmosphere. Of course, there was gambling going on everywhere, the noise of the cha-chings and coins spilling into trays making this city have its own kind of musical theme.

We were exhausted when we returned to the Holden. My hubby and I said goodnight to the in-laws, then went to our own room. Even though we were already sexually active there was newness to our journey. We played in our own room without fear of his family hearing us. We would jump on the bed. I got to try on my seductive nighties that made me feel more vulnerable than just being naked. We became very loud. The person next door kept pounding on the wall yelling at us to, "knock it off already!"

The next day, after sitting in for some meetings, the in-laws, my hubby, and I went to lunch. We explored the Holden a bit more. You seriously could live in this hotel without having to leave. It pretty much had everything. We decided to play a hand at some gambling machines. My hubby and I decided to just gamble 20 dollars. If we ran out, then we were done. He exchanged the money for coins and we played a few machines, winning five to ten dollars here and there. I was at this one machine that I played about four times. I was going to try just one more time when my hubby made me move to another machine. A man come behind me, put in a coin, and hit the jackpot, winning 5,000 dollars. I glared at my hubby with my mouth open in astonishment. I stated, "I could have won!" and then proceeded to give him a hard time. I still do, all in fun though. I lost a little bucket of coins. But, we didn't lose our money. We still came out with just a little more than what we started with.

As the weekend progressed, I found that my hubby and me were never without my in-laws, only late at night when we retired. I wasn't happy about this at first. A honeymoon is not supposed to be spent with others, especially parents. I decided to let it go, thinking my husband and I could get away for another weekend to have a real honeymoon. My husband's dad planned all the outings. They were fun. I figured that he just wanted to show us around because he's been here before. He liked to joke and tell funny stories. Near the end of the weekend I was getting a bit irritated that my hubby and I couldn't be alone. I tried to overlook it but it was getting hard. The weekend ended so fast, and we were soon flying home.

Once home we made plans for a reception at a Grange Hall, a building in the community, usually placed on a dirt road in the country, for rent to hold large gatherings and often used as a church. We invited family and friends. There were quite a few people, but not too many. It was just right. We had music, a wedding cake, and great food. Everyone seemed to be enjoying themselves. I felt at home, although I do believe I turned red a few times. There was dancing and laughter. I thought my life was just beginning. I felt I had purpose now, that my life finally had meaning, and that I had someone to share it with.

My hubby and I moved into a travel trailer that belonged to my dad. We lived in it on his parents' property, and I soon discovered his parents involved themselves in everything. No choice or decision was made without my father-in-law's approval. Soon after we got back I stopped going to church because my father-in-law, all of sudden, disapproved. I stopped working for Grandma because it was too overwhelming mixing her drama with my in-laws' drama. I became overwhelmed with in-laws and their disapproval in every area of my life. I'm surprised I was allowed to use the bathroom by myself. Before my hubby and I were married this family seemed like day, but after I married they seemed like night. My husband's attitude would change when around his dad. I thought for a long time that, "We should have waited longer. We should have found a place of our own." It was hard being 21 and finding myself being put in bondage under my in-laws. But I wasn't going to run from a difficult situation again.

I felt like an outsider in my new family. I struggled with anger and depression. I was losing my husband. I hated and resented my father-in-law. I felt helpless and didn't know what to do. I was falling, spinning out of control, with many negative emotions and actions surrounding me and consuming me.

11. THE BEGINNING OF DARKNESS

"And because lawlessness will abound,
The love of many will grow cold."
~Matthew 24:12

    I made the mistake of standing up to my father-in-law, who had power of strength, authority, and determination. I voiced my opinion on things. This was just not done. It was very hard to see or understand this being raised in a big family where everybody voiced their opinions. Voicing an opinion was basically, to me, a form of saying, "This is what I believe!" It didn't mean I thought any less of people with different views. But, in this family, it became obvious that they were very different. If you didn't think or believe the way they did, or I should say the way the dad did, then you were accused, judged, and then found guilty. The way I was raised was a strong force in my life. My father-in-law and I were consumed in friction toward each other. Ephesians 6:12 says, "For we do not wrestle against flesh and blood, but against principalities, against powers, against the rulers of the darkness of this age, against spiritual hosts of wickedness in the heavenly places." Evil forces were working against us.
    Three months into the marriage we went to a swap meet in Seattle. This is where I became pregnant with my first child. I took the opportunity to walk around with my husband. Things were not that bad just yet, but they were leading up to it. I was looking at everything and fell behind a couple of steps. I had never experienced a swap meet before and found it fascinating. There was so much stuff from vehicle parts, to clothing, and toys. I was enjoying the walk with my husband. I felt someone grab my hand, it was as if a shockwave of evil went up my arm. It could have been the strangeness of it, or the fact that some stranger would actually come and grab my hand.

But because of that surge I jerked my hand away and quickly walked up to my hubby, grabbing his hand for protection. I then looked behind me and was shocked to see it was my father-in-law. It was a strange experience. Putting myself in his shoes I can understand his hurt. But in a sea of people how could I have known it was him. This action further turned my father-in-law even more against me. If I was more mature I would have walked right back to him and apologized. I would have grabbed his hand and then walked with him a bit. But I didn't.

The in-laws were quickly coming in-between my husband and me. My husband withdrew from me because he was being attacked, in a bullishly teasing way, about being whipped by me and being told that I was controlling him. For someone who became tired of head games in the dating scene I married into a family that was pro at playing head games. I don't think my husband even saw what was happening. We didn't step back and look at the big picture. My husband wanted to make everyone happy, but in the process basically made no one happy. I, with my frustration of our marriage not being allowed to become what a marriage should be, was unable to see beyond my own emotions. We both realized what was happening a bit too late

Ben's younger brother Willy, one time, when we were running errands, decided he would steal the front seat when I was out of our vehicle. My hackles were already up about not being able to have a real marriage. I threw a bit of a fit. I was angry! My husband told his brother I wouldn't have an issue with it so he became mad at me for making him look bad. So, I sat in the back in quiet anger at how he was allowing his family to shove me aside. I see it now that his younger brother wanted to show that he still came first in his brother's life. He still does this even as an adult. I'm pretty sure that he complained to his dad about my fit of not being able to sit in the front. Afterwards, I basically was not allowed to sit in the front when going somewhere with one or more of my in-laws along. My husband allowed his family to come between us and above me by not wanting to deal with the hardship of confronting their anger or hurtful actions. He allowed them to cross lines that shouldn't be crossed.

With my husband being in the middle of five kids he was left out a lot. He wanted a relationship with his dad badly. He did anything to please a dad that was hard to please. My father-in-law used this to get what he wanted. My husband and I started fighting just because my father-in-law and I didn't see eye to eye. My attitude toward it all didn't help the situation either. But all I could see was that my in-laws deceived me, my husband didn't love me enough to stand up for me, and all the negative ways I was being treated. My in-laws were constantly with my husband and me. We never did anything on our own anymore. I began to feel that I married the family, not just my husband. I did marry into the family, but I did not marry the family. In this situation, I was becoming lost, confused, resentful, and angry. Proverbs 30:33

says, "For as the churning of milk produces butter, And wringing the nose produces blood, so the forcing of wrath produces strife." The strife in my life started to produce hatred.

My father-in-law also became mentally and verbally abusive. He took charge over who I could or could not see. I wasn't allowed to leave the property without his say so. My life was completely flipped inside out. I hated my life. For the first time, I started to hate someone else, and myself. The guilt of feeling these emotions would weigh on me. I have never hated before. I have strongly disliked but never hated. My face started getting frown lines. For someone who used to smile all the time I found days where I never smiled. I began to feel forgotten, useless, unworthy, and non-existent. I didn't matter. I prayed and prayed. I cried to God for help. I started sinking into my negative emotions. I started to feel that God wasn't even listening. I wasn't sure what to do. I did know that this marriage was important to me, that I wanted it to survive. But at the same time, I wanted to run away.

I often imagined knocking out my husband, tying him up, and throwing him in the vehicle, then packing up the stuff that we needed and disappearing from the in-laws. But that wouldn't have solved anything. Plus, my husband has a hard head, literally. I wouldn't be able to knock him out if I tried.

I did love and appreciate my mother-in-law. I could talk to her about some of the emotional struggles I was going through. She would give me advice in the areas that were affected by my father-in-law in a negative way. She helped me understand how my actions and word choice could put me at odds with him. Soon it became evident that my father-in-law just saw me as an enemy. He saw me as someone to change, wanting to form me into what he approved of. All his anger toward women, those who hurt him in the past, became anger toward me. It all was becoming more of an emotional struggle than I could handle. I soon became withdrawn and quiet.

While I was pregnant with my first child, this struggle was hard to go through. I remember being largely pregnant, looking like an umpa lumpa, with my feet aching and my back hurting. There were times when there was no place to sit and nobody would offer up a seat. I didn't want to ask because I didn't want to get lectured on how I was not special enough to have a place to sit. When I went to my grandma's for a family reunion, the last one I went to, one of my uncles offered me a seat, and I almost lost it and started balling. I sucked it up though because I didn't want to bring my problems out. I wanted to enjoy my visit. I was becoming disconnected with the world, putting on a brave face when I was dying inside.

I lost connection with all my friends. I was finding it hard to stay connected to family. My mom tried to get me to leave. I felt strongly that I should stay. I would often hear in my head, "Stay and be patient." I wanted to do what was right even if it was hard. I didn't want to deal with my father-in-law's hate. He was very negative and mean. Even as I knew I made the right choice, I started to let fear rule my life. The sun was no longer shining because I had a huge mountain blocking it, overshadowing me. Luke 11:34 says, "The lamp of the body is the eye. Therefore, when your eye is good, your whole body also is full of light. But when your eye is bad, your body also is full of darkness." My eye was filling with anger and hate; it was becoming bad. I was falling in darkness.

I started to pretend to be the person my father-in-law wanted me to be. There just seemed to be no other way. Even so, he still found something wrong with me. He was never pleased. I soon cherished the moments when I was alone at night with my hubby where I could be myself. Those times were what kept me going. I had chosen to love and marry him. I was determined to make this marriage work. I knew he loved me, though he had a false sense of duty toward his family out of the strong desire to find a connection. I did not understand this at first. I just held on to the hope that one day soon, things would change.

The day came when I went into labor with my first child. But the doctor working that night said that it was false labor, gave me a pill, and sent me home. A couple days later, the day after thanksgiving, I was having contractions again. The family joked that I ate too much holiday food and there was no room for the kid. My mother-in-law drove me in. My hubby showed up, having to miss out on a day of 'jeeping' in the mountains. This labor seemed to take forever. I became so exhausted that I just didn't want to be there anymore. My hubby encouraged me to push, push, push. I told him, "You push, push, push!" He laughed, I glared.

When nothing seemed to be happening but the pain I stated, "That's it I've had enough, I want to go home!" Everyone chuckled. Finally, our son was born. My body sighed in relief. The baby looked dark. I found out it was from lack of oxygen. He made it just in time. The doctor said I was going to have to push one more time for the placenta to come out. I groaned. I felt as though I didn't have another push in me.

After it all, I just wanted to sleep. At the hospital, I tried to fall asleep but found myself drifting in and out with the excitement of having a little new born son who was watching television with his dad so I could rest. Not long after, friends and family started to visit. I met my older sister-in-law for the first time. She came from Seattle to drop in and visit. My father-in-law came in and asked if it was worth it. Thinking of everything I went through and the precious little bundle my hubby was holding I said, "I would do it all over again." My father-in-law decided to take this as a rub-it-in-your-face statement. He still mocks me, saying in a ridiculing voice, "There, I'd do it again!" Then he would proceed to lecture me that I deserved the pain and that I don't know what's good for me.

Finally, we were able to go home. Our son was a very easy child. From the start, he would sleep all night. My breast milk never came in so we ended up bottle-feeding him. He was such a little cute cartoonish baby with his dark hair and dark blue eyes. As a new mother, I loved and appreciated the advice my mother-in-law gave me. About a week after my son was born, I had a dream I was peeing in the toilet. I felt warm liquid surround me. I instantly jumped out of bed and quietly ran to the bathroom. I could not believe I peed the bed. I didn't know what to do. I didn't want my father-in-law to find out. My mother-in-law swooped in after she woke up, took charge, and helped me figure it out before my father-in-law was up and moving around.

My favorite memory of sleeping on that bed was that it was really squeaky. Whenever we tossed and turned the bed squeaked loudly and my younger sister-in-law Sally in the next room would jump off her bed and stomp her feet to let us know she was still awake because she thought we were up to something. My hubby and I would laugh and squeak the bed some more on purpose. But, even with the good moments, because negativity was so strong in this family, darkness would creep in more and more, swallowing me bit by bit.

In the beginning, I tried to fight the negativity but it was much stronger then I was. I was one person standing alone in a group of strongly stubborn individuals. I soon found my light being snuffed out gradually from each verbal attack. I tried to reach out to God, but felt He wasn't there. I struggled with the understanding that He was there even if I couldn't feel Him. I found it hard to read the Bible. I was having a hard time knowing how to pray. I began to sink further and further into misery. I felt like a little bird trapped inside a dark cave underneath a gigantic mountain, flapping my wings trying to find freedom, running through deep tunnels seeking a place where I might break out into that freedom. I began to lose hope of seeing the light. I felt as though my father-in-law clipped my wings to keep me from flying.

12. AN ANGEL IN DISGUISE

"Unto the upright there arises light in the darkness;
He is gracious, and full of compassion, and righteous."
~Psalm 112:4

    I was filled with pain as my life became the very opposite of what I was used to. Instead of being free with my own desires, choices, and time, I was basically forced to live out their dreams, their choices, and their time. My life was no longer my own. Feeling forgotten, I was losing my own Identity. This is something that is very dangerous to do to a person. In this we lose everything that brings the light of life to us that made life worth living. We lose the will to fight to live.
    One day I was walking with my two-year-old son, pregnant with a second child, in downtown Friar River. I would often take a walk to check the mail. After the post office, I would slowly mosey on back to my husband's family business. I remember hoping to run into someone I knew, someone I haven't seen in a while. With having a child and with my other issues, my world was somewhat isolated. I felt lost, alone, and depressed when a woman approached me. Not knowing if I should know this person I hesitantly smiled. Taking the hand she offered, she looked me straight in the eyes and said, "I know you don't know me, but I had the strongest urge to come tell you that God has not forgotten you."
    I immediately became emotional, though I tried my hardest to hide it. I said, "thank you, I needed to hear that!" I truly did. Those days, in the beginning of loneliness and feelings of being forgotten, my emotions were very screwed up. I could start balling at the drop of a hat. I remember not wanting to show these emotions in public or to anybody. I liked being smiley, a happy go lucky, and an enjoyable person to be around. Not a tear bubbling,

face scrunching, freak show. Yes, this is what crying in front of someone makes me feel. It took all I had not to burst in front of this stranger. She probably could see all the emotions playing across my face, which probably looked just as silly. I truly needed to hear those words. First Thessalonians 5:11 says, "Therefore comfort each other and edify one another, just as you also are doing." God sent this woman to comfort and edify me, to give me a hope to hold onto.

The woman gave me a hug. She was a stranger spreading love. My soul was lifted. After she let go we parted. Continuing on, I reached my husband's family business. After getting my emotions and face under control, I entered. Just as I entered, Sally came in a few minutes later behind me and handed me a twenty dollar bill with some confusion, saying, "A woman stopped me, she said she just talked to you, and she asked me to give this to you." I became emotional again, though the money didn't matter. The words the woman spoke meant everything.

Sally stood there having the expression of, "what's wrong with you?" on her face. I told her about the nice lady with the much needed words. Then I received a second hug. Two hugs in one day, I was on a roll. Hugs were rare then. My in-laws were not a touchy, huggy family. Sally and I have had our spats and arguments but we understood each other. She knew I needed that hug. That wonderful lady didn't know how much those words would mean to me for the next ten years of my life, and neither did I. Life became so much harder and darker. Sometimes I was an emotional wreck, and other times I didn't feel anything. Those times were scary.

As I continued to live in this situation, loneliness was like a second skin to me. The funny thing is that I was hardly ever left alone. The loneliness was inside my soul. I didn't feel accepted or liked by the people around me. I could do nothing right. Everything I did offended my father-in-law. I was so tired of being alone. They probably thought I was crazy when I would often burst out singing the lyrics to "All by My Self," by Celine Dion—trying to lighten the mood and hoping they would get a hint. They never did! I tried to talk to my husband about it but it never seemed to get anywhere. He would often take their side. He often had me apologize for wrongs I wasn't sure I committed or understood. I did it because my husband asked it of me and to bring back some peace if possible. In all of this I felt misunderstood, mistreated, with no one willing to help. I was truly alone in this family.

With that decade of my life, I struggled with circumstances beyond my control, believing I was forgotten. This would lead to negativity and depression so deep that all I could see was darkness. But, when I was at my lowest those words would pop into my head, "God has not forgotten you." They would repeat over and over in my mind. Those words seemed to exist just for me, getting me through those difficult times. It brought life where death wanted to rule.

I don't even want to imagine what my life would have been like without those words. I wonder what caused that woman to have the urge to come speak to me. I must have looked miserable. I have never been able to hide my emotions well. I also wonder what my apparel must have looked like for her to feel the need to give me money. Whatever the reason that brought her to me, I will be forever grateful because the next years I felt like I was trapped in the middle of a category five tornado with the oxygen being sucked from my soul. I was crushed to the lowest place I could go. But with one phrase, a little love, and understanding from a stranger, I was able to keep holding on.

It makes my heart sing to know that there are people, even strangers, who care enough to act, speak out, and bring healing. This stranger inspired goodness and light to my soul. Though to this day, I still don't know who this person is and most likely will never know. I choose to see her as my angel in disguise. She gave me words that got me through my darkest hours, "God has not forgotten you."

13. SUICIDAL EMOTIONS

"For the enemy has persecuted my soul;
He has crushed my life to the ground;
He has made me dwell in darkness, like those who have long been dead."
~Psalm 143:3 (NKJV)

Dealing with my second pregnancy, I was often in tears. I was hoping for a girl. Like my first pregnancy, I had morning sickness really bad. With this pregnancy, we found a midwife who worked with us. She was also qualified to deliver babies at our community hospital. This was perfect for us. I was more comfortable having a woman, and so was my husband. She was amazing, and she also became a confidant. I would let things spill from deep within myself in her check-up room. It helped knowing that she went to my old church and was connected to my old friends, who I hadn't seen in years. I connected to this woman who would listen to me with understanding and love. She felt like family, something I haven't felt in a while. Abigail's mom worked as the receptionist there. Here, at the doctor's office, I felt at home. I looked forward to all my visits, even when I had to get the shots I hated.

My due date passed me by, and I was often taking walks up and down the road, doing squats, just to get this baby to decide to come out. The baby didn't want to budge. I should have taken this as a sign of how stubborn this kid would turn out to be. A week or two after the due date I started to have contractions. They weren't as bad as the first time. We called the mid-wife and then met her at the hospital. I was really hoping for a girl. But, another son was born. I felt angry that one more thing didn't turn out in what I was hoping for. Life was cruel. I didn't want to hold him. I started falling into depression even more. I understood it to be the beginning of Postpartum

Blues. I then became angry at myself. I knew that I was not going to be able to handle this type of depression with everything going on in my life right now. It would destroy me. My children would not have a mom to take care of them. I went to the source of my hurt feelings. The child couldn't help what it was. This was God's will. I prayed and asked for forgiveness for my anger and hurt. I reached into the little bed he was in, picked him up, and held him close. I told him, "I love you." I still say this to him when he's being stubborn and making me angry. He gets into trouble and then afterwards I tell him I still love him. He was my most difficult baby and is still my most difficult child so far.

My husband's older brother Mick started coming around with his family and kids. I ended up babysitting his three kids during the week at the shop while both parents went to work. It was nice to make a little extra money for groceries. We struggled financially. Let's just say working for family can create problems. The older brother moved his family to a house in town near the shop which allowed me to walk over and watch the kids at their house. I did as my mom taught me, doing the dishes and picking up the house. This always gave me a good reputation. I liked doing it. But, my father-in-law had his own ideas. I got into trouble for doing this for them. He lectured and yelled at me, "You don't need to do them any favors!" I was dumbfounded. I just started keeping what I did to myself.

Soon we moved out of the in-laws' house and back into a little camp trailer on the property with our two boys. They sold the shop in town and brought the business home. I figured this would be good, because then my hubby and I might be able to have more time together. That never happened. Not only did I get less time with him because everybody would show up after work to hang out at the shop. I never got a break from my father-in-law's verbal abuse. He was always around. When they were all together they would all turn on me. I had no champion. I tried to stay away, but that got me into trouble too. I found myself falling further and further down that black hole.

I started watching Mick's kids here. I had to be so careful on how I treated them, where I let them play, and how I would feed them. My father-in-law had his nose in everything. I was not allowed to punish the youngest boy because he was the favorite. He was also the worst behaved, always biting, hitting, and pulling his two older sisters' hair. He never listened. I got accused of playing favorites when I would get after him for this. Yes, he was a funny little dust monster but he would lose his temper fast. These kids, including my own two boys, soon became dubbed the brat pack. They were extremely stubborn and willful. They were always covered in poof dust from head to toe. I often took the broom to them before they came into the trailer. They hated the broom and I hated the dust. But this has become a memory we all laugh about. I watched these kids for a couple of years, and then one day their mother took them away. We didn't see them for years. They're mom's personality and my father-in-law's negativity and demands just wasn't working out. We all missed those kids.

One summer we went camping for a week. My hubby's older sister and her family went too. She was pregnant with her second child and loving the attention. I was so happy not to be pregnant. I didn't like the attention and hardships of being pregnant while living with this family. But, after we came home it hit me that I haven't had a period in a while. I went to my midwife and took the pregnancy test. It tested positive, but not only that, I was five months along. I had been so depressed and unhappy that the days ran together. I didn't listen to my own body. I was amazed that I didn't have morning sickness with this one. I didn't even feel pregnant. I knew it had to be a girl. The midwife asked me to pick a day for it to be born in April, so I picked the fourteenth. She said the mothers sometimes often know when the baby will come. I thought this was kind of crazy but went with it. That number felt good.

Nobody was really happy about the pregnancy, including myself. I didn't want to bring another kid into this unhappy family, although I was looking forward to it possibly being a girl. But either way I knew I was going to love the child.

Time seemed to fly. We had some new neighbors. A single mother with a couple kids who seemed nice. But everything went downhill fast. Some rumors started that I had sex with my husband's older brother while I was watching his kids at his house in town. Also, all of a sudden there were rumors that I was sexually active with some others that I didn't even know. Since I did not have my flower when Ben and I married my husband chose to believe these accusations. The actions of my past caused issues with my present and future. It was tearing my marriage apart.

Ben started getting interested in our neighbor. He said he just went there to have someone to talk to, but it was more than that. You could hear it in his voice when he answered her phone call. When she showed up he would light up for her like he used to for me. He started to spend time at her house, when he should've been spending time with me. All the sudden he didn't want me anymore because he thought I'd lied to him. That's when I told him everything that I did in my past and that I had nothing to do with any of his brothers. It was so hard, because I was so ashamed. I truly believed myself to be a virgin because I didn't go all the way. My husband was my real first.

This all continued for a couple of weeks. I was so distraught that it felt like the end of the world. My hubby was hurt, I was destroyed, and life just stopped. I felt that I had held onto this marriage just to have it fall apart by rumors and propaganda. I then found out that it was Mick who started it. My little brother-in-law Willy, the baby of the family, kept it going. They started many rumors. Willy told one of his friends to tell my husband that we dated, saying that my husband would get a big kick out of it. I confronted Willy's friend and asked him to please stop. That's when I found out about my little brother-in-law. Everything seemed to just fit together after that. I continued to watch this as Willy continued to play his games and create drama.

My husband finally told the neighbor girl it wasn't going to work. He saw the pain he was causing. He didn't want to be the cause of that pain. Also, he just wasn't the type to cheat even when he felt betrayed. He chose to work out our marriage. He told me it may take him a while to work out his feelings but he wanted to work it out. The neighbor girl soon found someone else. They also started a feud with my father-in-law. This took his attention off me for a little bit though. It just goes to show that first impressions are not always the true ones. People let you see what they want you to see, then turn on you when they don't get what they want. There's so much selfishness in this world. There's so much negativity and darkness. Where I stood it all seemed to be directed at me, drowning me in its gooey blackness.

In all this I went through my third pregnancy. Towards the end of this pregnancy I started leaking fluid. It wasn't much but I wore a pad so I didn't wet myself. I had no idea what this meant until I got involved with a book club where a girl had the same problem. She rushed herself to the hospital because it was fluid from the placenta. I decided to get checked out by my midwife, so I called her.

"That's not good, come over now so I can check you out right away," she said.

I quickly made it to her office, and sure enough, my placenta fluid was leaking a little. I went straight to the hospital. On my way there, I realized it was the fourteenth of April. Who would have thought? This pregnancy went extremely fast. I couldn't even feel the contractions except for the tightening of the skin. When it came time to push, the baby came out just after a couple of pushes. The umbilical cord was wrapped around the neck so they flipped the baby quickly to unwrap it. The baby was alright. She was a big healthy baby girl, almost ten pounds.

I was happy to have a girl since my hubby and I decided this would be our last. We had our two boys and a new baby girl while still trying to work out our marriage issues. My husband would go out with Willy to the bars, drinking and causing a ruckus. Willy tried hard to encourage my husband to cheat on me, something that just isn't in my husband's nature. I struggled in this because I lost some trust in him when he was visiting the neighbor girl. Yes, I made some choices in my past that weren't right. But I overcame and sought forgiveness. I changed my life around. But, these actions were being used against me. It doesn't matter if I made these choices way before my marriage. These choices still affected this present time and still can affect the future. They were negative actions that caused negative reactions. Even though I know that God has forgiven me and I changed my ways, there will still be those who will condemn and judge me—who will use those actions against me. Willy is one of these people. He had tried throughout the years to destroy our marriage.

Also, on top of this, my in-laws weren't getting close to our daughter for some reason. They say that it was because I kept her to myself, but I remember telling them if they wanted to spend time with her to just say so. I felt as though my father-in-law held it against me because I had a girl. There were a lot of up and down emotions during this time. With each up, the down went further, which brought me lower and lower.

My hubby and I soon worked things out over my past, but it still would come up every so often. Although this was a step forward, I soon found myself the subject of ridicule, hate, and accusations.

My world became limited in a restricted and controlled situation. I no longer had a vehicle. My father-in-law provided a phone for me but I was not allowed to use it to communicate with the outside world. I was only allowed to use it within my husband's family. Somewhere in all this I became afraid. I feared my father-in-law. Fear and hate pulled on me with a strength that I was too weak to fight. This negativity took away what little of myself I had left. Our family had grown. I loved my husband and children with all my heart, yet I continually walked in a negative bubble, allowing all the hurtful actions and hateful words to bring me down further and further into a deep depressed place. I was surrounded by gray fog with only a sliver of light breaking through. I was falling deeper into feeling worthless, unwanted, unloved, lost, and insecure. I wondered what the point of living was. I wanted to end my life. Psalm 88:3 says it perfectly, "For my soul is full of troubles, and my life draws near to the grave."

My in-laws took over the decision-making regarding my children. I felt as though I was just a nanny making sure they didn't get hurt, ate their meals, and got some sleep. I had no say in anything. In those days, I found myself in tears. I cried every day. I thought about leaving. I didn't want to leave my kids or my husband. I started to pray, asking God for guidance. I continued to feel a whisper in my mind telling me to stay, to be patient. So, this is what I did. I suffered through the day-to-day verbal abuse.

One day I'd had enough and walked off alone, praying to God, crying out from within my soul, "God would you please find me a place to hide out!" Some weeks later my husband came home pulling a longer trailer with a tip out and two bedrooms that had big bubbly letters that said Hideout. I was in awe. I asked and I received. We moved from the small cramped trailer into the larger one. It felt like a mansion. I was hoping things would start changing but they didn't. Our living situation may have changed a little but I was still in darkness. I would try to avoid my in-laws but my father-in-law would get mad at not seeing me for a while. When I would visit, he would always find something offensive about me, even when I was trying to be nice.

This discouraged me from wanting to try at all.

I soon became tired of feeling alone. I was tired of being helpless, worthless, and feeling like I didn't matter to anyone. I fell deeper into suicidal depression. I struggled with this for a while. I no longer wanted, but felt I had to end my life. I would tell myself that it wasn't right. Committing suicide was a sin. It was wrong to destroy something God had brought to life. I would tell myself that my kids needed me, even though I believed they didn't. I didn't think my husband would miss me. We never did anything together anymore. He was always doing stuff with his family and friends, leaving me behind.

I tossed and turned with this struggle for weeks. Then a day came when I was sitting on our bed, with tears of frustration and a demanding desire to end it all. I stared at my husband's gun, which I grabbed from the table on his side of the bed. There were no bullets in or around the gun, due to my husband, a smart man. I will never forget that overwhelming emotion of wanting it all to end. It was a force that pulled me. I believed in God and that suicide was wrong, but the emotional pull was very strong. Since I couldn't find any bullets I thought of using a knife to slit my wrists. As I seriously contemplated this action I started thinking of my faith, husband, and children. I thought of what they meant to me and what I meant to them. The love I have for these three sent a ray of light to pierce the black cloud I was sitting in. I focused on this love, this sliver of light, and it grew. I realized that what I was contemplating was selfish, that this was a hateful action, and it would bring more harm than good. My faith forbade it, my husband loved me, and my children needed me. I thought about all the hugs with my children, the times my husband came in and cuddled me. I knew there was love. It was just hiding in the dark cloud of negativity. I sighed, knowing that I could never take my own life even though I greatly desired it. Just the same, this day changed my life forever. Hitting bottom showed me that I have a choice. I chose to be less selfish and more selfless. I chose to stop hating and to give love. Psalm 112:4 says "Unto the upright there arises light in the darkness; He is gracious, and full of compassion, and righteous." God pulled me out of darkness with the light of his love.

Proverbs 10:12 says, "Hatred stirs up strife, But love covers all sins." I realized that I was being consumed by my own hate. The darkness that surrounded me was caused by myself. Yes, my circumstances sucked. But I was only a victim if I allowed myself to become one. I started to grow into a maturity of love. I took my first step by making the choice to love and not hate. Acting out like I did revealed hatred for my father-in-law, but also for myself. In this act of choosing to break free of hate, I was given the understanding that our negative emotions swarm around trying to consume us, not wanting to let us go. They try to keep us boxed in. Negativity wants to keep us bound, lost in a world of lies and deceit. But, the good news is we have a choice and we can break free. I did. I turned from the dark shadows. My soul sang of this change.

Once I broke free I could see beyond my negativity. I no longer had the suicidal emotions. Instead of a black world I was surrounded by color and beauty with bright light. My circumstances may not have changed but I did. I changed where it counts, deep within. I started a journey of discovering true love.

14. REDISCOVERING LOVE'S TRUE MEANING

*"The night is far spent, the day is at hand.
Therefore let us cast off the works of darkness, and let us put on the armor of light."*
~Romans 13:12 (NKJV)

    I decided to restudy the meaning of love. I chose to study everything I could on the subject, even the stuff I already was taught from Sunday school and church. I looked at the different types of love for different relationships. There is love between husband and wife, mother and children, and between father and children. Then there is the sisterly love, brotherly love, and love between friends. There are so many different versions. It's a wonder my head stayed on straight.

    I opened my Bible, knowing that I had a lot to study. This journey was going to take time. I mentally erased everything I thought I knew about love and gave myself a clean slate. My eyes were open and my mind began to grasp that true love can be for anyone. In fact, we should have it for everyone because it should come from ourselves, not others. God is love and since we are created in His image, we have the capacity to receive love and give love. We can go look for true love, but we won't find it because we're looking in the wrong place. I saw myself in the past as a person who kept searching and searching. I didn't find it in someone or something else. I may have thought I found true love in my past relationships, but eventually the other person let me down or I let the other person down. And as the relationship got older the feelings faded and just disappeared, I lost the love I once had. This also goes for materialistic love. I saw before me a picture of everlasting love, a love that doesn't come and go. This view of love is beautiful.

    I started to understand that some people may try to find love in sex, which could actually be just lust. Some with many partners because they're afraid of commitment to just one person, afraid to give their hearts away because they might get broken. But that's not love. There are so many ways that we try to find love. But there is only one way to find true love.

As I kept studying I began to see a whole new side. Where does God reside? In us. So, if God is love, love's truest form comes from within me. It doesn't work to try to find love from others. That is what I now see as selfish desire. I was quite greedy and needy in that aspect. I had been suffocating in my need of love, scared that I could lose it if I gave it space. Love should be freely given, or it's not love at all. I began to understand with clarity that love comes from me, not others. It is giving of myself, not seeking it in others. I realized that I didn't need to care about how people viewed me. I needed to care about how I treated others, including my father-in-law. I prayed asking forgiveness for the lies I believed about love. I prayed for God to give me love for my father-in-law. I felt a release—a bondage broken. I was set free from the curse that held me bound.

I tried an experiment. I closed my eyes as I focused and meditated on the center of my chest where my heart is. I felt the glow of love that resides there and saw that it's an energy that resides in my soul. I pictured it flowing from myself. I felt that I had an endless supply, so I didn't need to be stingy with it. A little spilt here or there is not going to hurt anybody. Not even those who are hard-hearted and can be cruel. My demeanor changed.

When I was up and around people, I began to let it flow to them. I began to love them with innocent actions or words without expecting anything in return. To do something good for someone made me feel good. I felt complete when the good I did put a smile on the other person's face. I have learned that it's not about what I get but what I give- what goes around comes around. If I give love I will be sure to get love. If I try to contain it, I will snuff it out like a flame without oxygen. I need to let the oxygen flow

Now that I had a picture in my head what love looked like I considered its meaning. 1 Corinthians 13:4-8says, "Love suffers long and is kind, love does not envy, love does not parade itself, is not puffed up, does not behave rudely, does not seek its own, is not provoked, thinks no evil, does not rejoice in iniquity, but rejoices in truth; bears all things, believes all things, hopes all things, endures all things. Love never fails." True love never fails, enduring all things no matter how difficult or hard.

It may not be very easy to love everyone, but when I got the hang of it, loving made life easier and well worth it. I began to direct love outward toward others, not inward. I started to understand that love does not always have to be a feeling. It can be an act of kindness, an encouraging word, and a helping hand. I saw that I can even show love to those I don't like. Matthew 5:43-48 tells us, "You have heard that it was said, 'You shall love your neighbor and hate your enemy.' But I say to you, love your enemies, bless those who curse you, do good to those who hate you, and pray for those who spitefully use you and persecute you."

I fell short on the verse Matthew 5: 43-48 most of the time. I usually have tried to hide from the people I don't like. I have said prayers for them, which probably is enough in some instances, but isn't enough in others. I needed to act in love also. I didn't try to not like anyone in particular. I ended up not liking certain people because they are difficult to be around or because they didn't like me. I'm sure there are many excuses used to justify not liking someone. As I started to put Matthew 5 into action I found that it released me from the bondage of the enemy. My in-laws' hate, spitefulness, and persecution rolled off me like beads of water.

I started praying for God to bless my enemies. I knew God loved them so I should show some act of love too. We are all human and we will clash. Our feelings get in the way. So will selfishness, greed, anger, and especially jealousy. But, I will remember, love isn't only feeling; it's acting. I can choose to act loving even if I don't feel it. I started to act loving toward my father-in-law. This wasn't easy at first. I began in a very timid way.

I read Matthew 5:38-42, which says, "you have heard that it was said, 'an eye for an eye and a tooth for a tooth.' But I tell you not to resist an evil person. But whoever slaps you on your right cheek, turn the other to him also. If anyone wants to sue you and take away your tunic, let him have your cloak also. And whoever compels you to go one mile, go with him two. Give to him who asks you, and from him who wants to borrow from you do not turn away." I put this into action. Every time my father-in-law wanted something done I worked hard at it with a glad heart. I now often get frustrated when I see quotes that say, "Get rid of the negative people in your life!" or "Leave the people that bring you down!" God allows people in our lives for a reason. I wouldn't have become the strong, loving person that I am without my father-in-law. I would not have grown to overcome and be strong in negative circumstances. I thought of Queen Esther from the Bible and the negative circumstances surrounding her. When Haman the Agagite stood against her and her people she didn't run, but instead stood her ground in love for her people. I took courage from this.

I believe Matthew 5:38-42 may be one of the hardest verses to follow. But this is the true form of an act of love. No feelings need be involved. In fact, I tended to go the other way. I wanted to stomp my feet, yell or scream, fight back, or just say no and ignore my in-laws. But after the new realization of acting in love I looked for ways to help and be patient. I found myself apologizing for misunderstandings without my husband telling me to. I know I won't always get it right, but I will give it my best. God will help if I ask, and I did just that!

Loving enemies will always be the hardest thing to do. But who am I to hate? Especially if God in all his glory loves me enough that He sent his son as a sacrifice for all my sins. He did this for everyone. God doesn't play favorites.

As I kept reading the Bible I learned that discipline, given in the right way, is an act of love also. But, we must be careful not to turn discipline into abuse. That is not done out of love, but out of anger and hate.

One day I came across a verse about punishment that I ended up loving. Matthew 23:37-39 says, "O Jerusalem, Jerusalem, the one who kills the prophets and stones those who are sent to her! How often I wanted to gather your children together, as a hen gathers her chicks under her wings, but you were not willing! See! Your house was left to you desolate; for I say to you; you shall see me no more till you say, 'Blessed is he who comes in the name of the Lord.'" God removed His presence, letting them know He will be there for them when they chose to accept Him and those He sent. That is an act of love.

I thought back to how love is patient and long suffering. No matter how long I struggle with difficulties, I need to love. No matter how long I wait for someone to get their act together, I need to be there for them when they decide they need me. This brings to mind the prodigal son, the story found in Luke 15: 11-32. To be able to let go and be there for people when they come back. I have seen people in frustration and anger lash out and seek vengeance. They throw up their hands and disown the people who frustrate them, whether they are relatives or friends. I have also watched people at the other end feel the loss, lose hope and become suicidal. If they have an ounce of hope that they can come to someone else with their struggles, knowing that someone loves them, those people might be saved from their downfall. With my isolation, I may not have had anyone, but I had three huge factors that kept me from taking that leap into the afterlife. I had God, love for my family, and the love from my family. Keeping love, which God has placed in us from people, is just wrong. It's in us to share. I also learned that we need to accept the love we are given. Sometimes we don't feel love because we aren't accepting it.

I came across my favorite chapter in the Bible, in this chapter I read the verse Romans 12:9-21 (NKJV), "Let love be without hypocrisy. Abhor what is evil. Cling to what is good. Be kindly affectionate to one another with brotherly love, in honor giving preference to one another; not lagging in diligence, fervent in spirit, serving the Lord; rejoicing in hope, patient in tribulation, continuing steadfastly in prayer; distributing to the needs of the saints, given to hospitality."

"Bless those who persecute you." Notice that this comes up again. Maybe because we are lack in doing this. "Bless and do not curse." My eyebrow is raised. I'm feeling that someone is trying to prove His point. I get it. "Rejoice with those who rejoice, and weep with those who weep. Be of the same mind toward one another. Do not set your mind on high things, but associate with the humble." Let's face it, if we set our minds on high things, we start thinking we are better then everyone, and lord things over them, which will cause friction and hate. "Do not be wise in your own opinion."

"Repay no one evil for evil. Have regard for good things in the sight of all men." Find the good in things and don't focus on the bad- "If it is possible, as much as depends on you, live peaceably with all men." There are those who we just cannot please, no matter what we do. "Beloved, do not avenge yourselves, but rather give place to wrath; for it is written, 'Vengeance is mine, I will repay,' says the Lord. Therefore, 'if your enemy is hungry feed him; if he is thirsty, give him drink; for in so doing you will heap coals of fire on his head.'" Now, I don't think this means to go, "Here have food and drink so your head might burn." We still need to be in the mind frame of showing love. Then give the rest up to God. "Do not be overcome by evil, but, overcome evil with good." I think this is where we all struggle. We get so overcome by emotions and feelings that they tend to rule our reactions. The way they cause us to react is not always the best.

I used to think that this was so impossible. I began to see that love is a lot about acting it out, whether we want to or not. But if we have God then we have the love to carry it through, to fight the dragons and climb the mountains. Not just for ourselves, but for others. As I put this into practice I saw how possible the impossible was.

Romans 8:35-36 shows how deep and everlasting love is. How nothing can take His love from us.

"Who shall separate us from the love of Christ? Shall tribulation, or distress, or persecution, or famine, or nakedness, or peril, or sword? As it is written: 'For your sake we are killed all day long; we are accounted as sheep for the slaughter.' Yet in all these things we are more than conquerors through Him who loves us. For I am persuaded that neither death nor life, nor angles, nor principalities, nor powers, nor things present nor things to come, nor height nor depth, nor any other created thing, shall be able to separate us from the love of God which is in Christ Jesus our Lord."

No matter what I went through, love was there. I struggled with depression, was even suicidal, but love was still there. I just had to call out to God and burst my negative bubble. I had to find it in myself through God. I had to stop looking for it in others. Looking for love in others builds expectations. All expectations got me was disappointment that became very dangerous. But, as I accepted the love that God freely gave to me I found it easier to give. It became the best gift that has ever been given to me besides the words, "God has not forgotten you."

Love covers all. As I kept growing in love it helped me through my struggles. It helped me see past my own faults and others' faults as well. It helped me be forgiving of myself and others, which saved my relationships.

If I didn't forgive people, then I would block the love flow. Think of it as the pay-it-forward theory. If our action and choices are good and loving toward others, without realizing it, we are causing a ripple effect that will continue on and come back.

I recall how I was confused about who I was and where my life was headed. I realized that I didn't need to worry about the choices I made as long as the choices were sound and didn't lead me down a path of destruction! Life is filled with dumb and bad choices. Those choices are not going to separate me from true love. I just needed to learn from mistakes and move on. We are all growing and learning. Our love can grow and learn too. I have learned that it hurts more to close myself off. It not only hurt me but others too. I closed myself off to friendships that would have been good, and the people who were close to me ended up fading away. I got hurt because I was afraid of getting hurt. My in-laws struggled with this just the same as me. Even though we had some of the same issues it was like a magnet turned backwards pushing us away from each other rather than pulling us close. It can become a vicious cycle repeating over and over. That is no way to live.

As I kept learning, discovering true love in myself gave me confidence and stability that we all strive for. This didn't only affect me but those around me. It also affected my own mental state of mind. I became less of the needy, weak person I once was. I grew in mental and spiritual strength and determination.

1 Corinthians 13:13 explains, "And now abide faith, hope, and love, these three; but the greatest of these is love."

Love is not always a feeling. Love is often an act of serving others. This made it easy to practice, and practice makes perfect! It's amazing how much joy I acquired from acting in love. When it becomes truly from the heart—and it did, it felt like I had wings to fly again. I learned this all with my father-in-law. No matter how he felt about me or treated me I found love for him. When I was being a push-over and somebody to walk on just to please people, it was not done out of love but out of a need to be accepted, which is why it hurt badly when I wasn't accepted. In love, I accept myself and I can stand up for what is right and just in the eyes of God.

15. MARRIAGE AND RELATIONSHIPS

"And the Lord God caused a deep sleep to fall on Adam, and he slept;
and He took one of his ribs, and closed up the flesh in its place.
Then the rib which the Lord God had taken from man He made into a
woman,
and He brought her to the man.
And Adam said, 'This is now bone of my bones, and flesh of my flesh;
She shall be called Woman, because she was taken out of Man.'
Therefore a man shall leave his father and mother and be joined to his wife,
and they shall become one flesh.
And they were both naked, the man and his wife, and were not ashamed."
~ Genesis 2:21-25

Last night I wanted to scream at my husband but just ended up glaring at him. I wanted to get some pizza and watch a movie with the kids but he refused. He let me carry on with my frustration. I might have slammed a cupboard or two while trying to figure out dinner. I kept asking him, "What do you want me to make?" With a shrug, he kept answering, "I don't know." This was driving me crazy.

A half hour later a vehicle pulled into the driveway and Ben jumped out of the trailer. It turns out he'd ordered pizza to be delivered. He'd had one too many beers and didn't want to drive. I felt bad about how I'd reacted, and at the same time my heart melted. When he came in with the pizza he looked at me and knew exactly what was going on in my head without me saying a word. I may not have had a marriage in the traditional sense since my husband didn't leave his parents, but we have become one. We're not ashamed in our nakedness together. We are not ashamed in our spiritual nakedness with each other. We now live in truth and honesty with each other even when we're not in the right. We can tell each other everything, even if it's difficult. I love this about my marriage. Ben has become an eagle in my life. He is straight and true. He doesn't play the head-games that his family has played. Our marriage may have started off awful and with many hardships, but we have come through the fire as refined silver. We're not perfect, but have accepted our imperfections. No relationship will be perfect.

When the right person comes along emotions will be united. Both hearts will have met and start to beat in unison. But, words of warning, "Just because it got started doesn't mean it won't stop!" The beginning of a relationship or marriage can feel like a fairytale. Ben and I seemed perfect together. We were made for each other. We would be together forever. But soon into our marriage, with life in between, the feelings faded. We didn't feel things much anymore. Instead of being happy to do things for each other, it became a chore. We lost the magic. One of my spiritual mothers once gave me good advice, even though I didn't completely understand it while learning it in purity class. She told me, "The right man could become the wrong man and the wrong man could become the right man." It doesn't matter which one we choose, it's the way we live and treat each other that defines our relationship. How we work past our issues. Marriage is hard work. What I've learned is that its survival depends on our willingness to let go and move forward, being honest, and choosing to forgive.

The choices Ben and I made in our relationship affected us both. Our actions caused a reaction in each other. In everything we did we needed to realize the other would be affected. We made choices that hurt and caused walls to be built up against each other. This is how the magic was destroyed. So, whether Ben and I were in the right or wrong, it comes down to how much we wanted our relationship to work. Did we have true love to overcome the hardships that did come? Some advice: overcome the hardships and the circumstances in your relationship that your choices have created. Don't ruin a relationship just because you don't like the circumstances. Circumstances will change. Don't run from your problems, you will only find more problems, unless the problems are extremely severe, like being physically abused. Then you have a true reason to run.

Perfection can become boring. I needed the struggles and mountains to add spice and adventure. I needed the highs and lows in my marriage to grow and to know how great the accomplishment is. Fighting and overcoming my problems in my relationship with Ben makes our relationship stronger and healthier. If I wouldn't have completed the story, I would have left it hanging. I wouldn't have allowed my character to grow. I wouldn't have allowed my and Ben's relationship to grow. I would have created a habit of continually running. It sounds tiring to me. When I climbed, at least I was heading to a resting point at the top of a mountain with a glorious view. I wasn't stuck at the bottom or in the middle going in circles.

I have heard many people say they need a relationship to be happy. I have learned that happiness isn't a relationship. If you enter a relationship while already happy and content, there is room for the relationship to grow into a healthy friendship. Life moves on and a relationship can face struggles and hardships, but when a relationship is healthy, these hardships and struggles aren't so hard to climb. When I got rid of my expectations of what I believed love was and accepted the love that is given, realizing that this might be the only way they know how to give love, I felt loved. In doing this my relationship with my husband and in-laws grew.

When I demand love then I don't feel like I'm getting it because my expectations are not being met, this will cause me to close up and get angry. I will end up causing the other person, who is giving all he or she knows how to give, to feel hopeless. This person will get angry which will turn into depression. They will start to see that the relationship is not worth trying anymore. This in turn will create walls on both sides. I won't let the other person get closer because my demands are not met, and the other person stops trying to get close because the feeling of not getting anywhere. We both will drift apart. I have created an obstacle that stops our journey up the mountain. This is what I went through with my father-in-law. I became hopeless because I couldn't meet his demands. I became frustrated because my own demands weren't being met.

With all my demands and expectations, I caused negative friction in my and Ben's relationship, as well as the relationship between my father-in-law and me. The reason I had demands and expectations was because of my own insecurities caused by past hurts. I needed to first deal with those hurts, to confess them, acknowledge the pain and repent, being sorry for my own actions and emotions. I had regret, I changed my feelings and mind, and I owned up to my part and changed the negative course to a positive direction. Then, the big one, I forgave. I let go, dropping all debts, imagined or real. This doesn't mean just for those who hurt me, but I also forgave myself as well. In doing these steps I broke down the walls blocking my path, allowing me to move forward up the mountain. This allowed my relationships to improve, grow, and become healthy. I crumbled the obstacles, freeing myself to continue my climb.

That was just the beginning. Relationships can and will get more complicated because of what we invest into the relationship, emotionally or physically. Touching base with my friends again, I discovered that the people who I thought would last forever are no more and some I didn't think would make it are still going strong. I began to see that no matter who I chose to spend my life with, my life would change and so would my relationships. I needed to be able to change with life and learn to be flexible. I needed to give and take, giving until I'm given to and then taking with love and appreciation.

I saw that I could be so selfish in my relationships. I thought what I was fighting for in the past was good and right. But what I was fighting for were earthly truths, not godly truths. I began to study the couples around me. I saw couples trying to take and take without giving in return. I saw them arguing and fighting over everything. No relationship is going to survive that, especially nowadays when it's so easy to quit and break up.

As I looked into what would make a relationship healthy in Godly terms, I discovered so many lies that have covered themselves as truths. In the beginning of a relationship people often confuse true love with those first feelings, the romance and the electricity we feel for each other. Those are great to have in a relationship but shouldn't define a relationship. A relationship is so much more complicated. Feelings are not always the good ones. True love comes from showing actions. Have you ever heard the saying, "Actions speak louder than words?" Let our actions of true love speak louder than our words of love. Some actions would be to keep your promises, to stand up for the other person, to give a helping hand even if it appears not to be needed, to make sure the physical and emotional needs are met, and Ben ordering a pizza when I'm throwing a bit of a fit. It means a lot when Ben does his best.

A marriage or relationship is more than feelings; it is a partnership. It's not about what we can get out of it, but it's about teamwork. That doesn't mean we can't have tons of good feelings and lots of romance. That is the magic that makes the relationship exciting and special. But it won't always be like that. Marriage life can be extremely hard. But if we have true love in us, we will always be able to work together through those hard times. I know that some might have true love and the other doesn't, and that it's not always our choice in which direction the relationship will go. Sometimes, no matter how hard we try to save the relationship, it's just not enough. At least we try. That should count for something. So many things can go wrong in a marriage. We just need to do our best.

My marriage's poor start caused negativity to steam-roll over us. With negative actions, there were negative and hateful reactions. It never became better until I put a stop to the negative and chose to act positive with acts of love. My marriage was saved because my husband and I chose to love against all odds. If we kept on the path of negativity we may have divorced. Things can go so wrong when we allow our emotions to rule. I believe some of the things that go wrong in a relationship are due to a lack of communication and from forcing the other to change. People will not change unless they want to change. Also, fighting to get the upper hand instead of meeting in the middle, being too controlling, putting family or friends before our spouse or significant other, and the worst—people who come in-between the two of us—can ruin a marriage. Relatives are very good at this, especially parents and in-laws who can't let go of parenting their kids and allow them to make their own choices. These situations can be very stressful and traumatizing for a marriage.

Genesis 2:24 and Mathew 19:3-6 says, "Therefore a man shall leave his father and mother and be joined to his wife and they shall become one."

When my children are grown, I pray that I will be strong enough to let them and their spouses have space. A parent myself, I know it is hard to let go. This doesn't mean I won't give advice. But I'll let them choose their path. I will let them know I will always be there when they need me.

It's good to get back to the basics of marriage and relationships. That with all the technology and the fast pace life has become we don't take time to step back and reevaluate our circumstances and relationships with each other. These things are not as complicated as we make them. It has been good to take a step back and slow down, to smell the roses. If life is allowed to go at a fast pace, it can spiral out of control. I would have loved a honeymoon after Ben and I married. But regardless, we found a strong foundation to stand on. When I come across people on the way to married-land, I will strongly suggest that they take their first year and make it all about each other. Let their heart and souls shine in each other and pretend no one else exists.

Genesis 2:18 explains, "It is not good that man should be alone; I will make a helper comparable to him."

The word "comparable" means we are able to be compared. We are similar and opposite where it counts. We were made male and female to complete each other. We both, male and female, being similar having strength in areas where the other lacks. We are like pieces of a puzzle that make a perfect fit. This is why I believe the opposite attracts. If we were the same piece of the puzzle we wouldn't fit. But, to be the opposite we can complete each other in personality, in our strengths and weaknesses, and also in our emotions. Ben has been my strength where I have been weak. He has showed me areas where I needed to improve. I have been his support. I have encouraged and stayed by his side even in all our difficulties. We have found a balance of give and take that works for us.

We may fit like a piece of a puzzle but that isn't all that a marriage needs to survive. It needs structure. Without a good foundation, anything will crumble—no matter how pretty it looks. People often think they can go into a marriage without changing their lifestyle, but, "News flash!" Life will change, some more dramatic than others. The Bible gives us this advice:

Ephesians 5:22-25 says, "Wives submit to your husbands, as to the lord. For the husband is the head of the wife, as also Christ is the head of the church; and He is the savior of the body. Therefore, just as the church is subject to Christ, so let the wives be to their own husbands in everything. Husbands, love your wives, just as Christ also loved the church and gave himself to her, that he might sanctify and cleanse her with the washing of water by the word, that he might present her to himself a glorious church, not having a spot or wrinkle or any such thing, but that she should be holy and without blemish. So husbands ought to love their own wives as their own bodies; he who loves his wife loves himself. For no one ever hated his own flesh, but nourishes and cherishes it, just as the Lord does the church… nevertheless let each one of you in particular so love his own wife as himself, and let the wife see that she respects her husband."

    I can hear and picture a lot of female emotional cries in rebellion and frustration. Me too! I've wanted to call the shots. I have believed several times that I knew best. But, if we put into place a structure for our relationships they will work a lot more smoothly. It shouldn't be about who needs to be on top or calling the shots. Men are to be the heads of the home, not because it's sexist or unfair, but because they're meant to be the protectors and providers. It's built into a man to protect his family from the dangers of this world and to provide, just as emotions are built into women for nurturing. This doesn't mean that the man should abuse this right and lord it over his wife. Thinking on this, I considered how Jesus treats the church, His bride. He didn't lord his position over them, He gave what people asked for if it was for the greater good. He made sure all needs were met. He listened, had compassion, and showed forgiveness. His church (the bride) respected Him by heeding his words, seeking Him out for advice, and putting Him first. We need to be able to work together in making decisions. A husband and wife are no longer two but one unit. Remember this is based on the bible and not my own opinion. Those who believe know where I'm coming from and those who don't believe in the Bible and are still reading on, I guess the best counsel I can give is find a structure that works best for you and your spouse.

    Another thing that is essential to a successful marriage is commitment. When Ben and I were saying our vows, we were committing to each other. We were making promises. These promises are the glue that hold the foundation together. If we can keep our commitment and promises, then we are trustworthy. I know not all promises are able to be kept, but depending on the circumstances, this doesn't mean you will lose the trust. Ben has promised dinner out but someone pulled up needing help with a vehicle. This broken promise is understandable. Trust, promises and commitment are all needed in a relationship for it to be a good relationship and survive.

    I guess a relationship can continue without these things, but I know it won't be a good relationship. A strong relationship needs trust. I have absolute trust in my husband even though he didn't keep all of his promises. He would promise family time but things would happen or people showed up that prevented it from happening. I used to get so mad at this but realized that I was not in control, and those people felt they needed a relationship with Ben too. Although he has broken his promises, he's faithful. There have been girls after girls who have literally thrown themselves at him, being such a handsome man, but he has remained faithful. There was this one girl who showed up to have her jeep worked on and stayed over a few days. She kept throwing herself at Ben. She even had the boldness to go up to Ben and tell him she had feelings for him. She stated, "I know you're married and I don't want to start anything but I don't know what to do with these feelings." I was so amazed by her choice of words. If she didn't want to cause problems, then she would not have said anything! I struggled with girls chasing Ben at first because of our past, but I realized that he loves me and respects me enough to cherish me in his faithfulness. I knew he was trustworthy.

Unfaithfulness will break the trust faster than anything else. This doesn't just mean cheating, which is the worst, but this also means lying, breaking promise after promise, or just being cold. None of these things are done out of love. Once trust is broken it will put a tear in the foundation that will be very hard to patch back up. Most of the time the tear will just keep growing until it destroys the foundation all together. Once the foundation is gone, the marriage or relationship can and will crumble. So, with that, we need to try hard not to lose the trust that has been given to us.

A foundation, trust, and commitment are very important to a relationship and marriage. This sounds boring but a relationship does not have to be boring. This is where romance comes in. Romance is very important in a marriage also. My and Ben's marriage is whatever we choose it to be. If we want comedy in a relationship, then give it a funny bone. A relationship and or marriage is what we make it. We will have our highs and lows but, no matter what we go through, if we have a strong foundation we will survive.

Ben and I need to find ways to have adventure and do things out of the norm. We need to break habits and be spontaneous once in a while. Ben is a very habitual creature. He will get into a routine and it's hard to break him out of it. We need to make time for each other where it's just the two of us beyond TV time in the evenings. I will start talking to him on purpose to drive him crazy while I rub his feet. Ben and I have a million little ways to show our appreciation for each other. I know if we do our best to try to keep the romance, we will. Everything takes work. Nothing will survive and move forward on its own.

16. RELATIONSHIPS WITH FAMILY AND FRIENDS

*"Be kindly affectionate to one another with brotherly love,
in honor giving preference to one another; not lagging in diligence,
fervent in spirit, serving the Lord; rejoicing in hope,
patient in tribulation,
continuing steadfastly in prayer; distributing to the needs of the saints,
given to hospitality."*
~Romans 12:10-13

    Waking up this Mother's Day morning I'm not sure what to expect. I have mixed emotions. I want to enjoy the day but know it will not be easy. I try to not have any expectations but they are there. These expectations will bring me down and I know they will. I get up with a sigh and start breakfast of bacon, hash browns, eggs, and pancakes. Soon my kids are up wishing me a happy Mother's Day. I smile and say, "Thank You." I get hugs from all of them. After breakfast is over, and Ben is out the door to his parents' house, all heck breaks loose. The kids start fighting. My frustration is building while I'm trying to keep calm as I start my morning chores. I finally snap and chase them out. I already feel like crying. Knowing I'm also going to have to face my father-in-law's hurtful words later, I start thinking of what I studied on relationships with family and friends. I thought about how we can treat each other and how we should treat each other. Like marriage, family and friendship also needs a good foundation and trust. The only difference in a friendship is you are not bound by a commitment. This doesn't mean we can't commit to our family and friends, though. Family can be by blood or by choice, and friends are people who we enjoy being around. We are close to them because we want to be. I do my best to be friends with my father-in-law but it's not easy at all. Any relationship will take work. In any relationship, we need to meet needs and give of ourselves.

I have had friends come and go, and some continue to stay in my life. I know some will be my friends forever. But no matter where I'm at in my friendships, whether we have become distant or close, we have been blessed to have a friendship. We need to treat each other like the gift our friendship is. It has always driven me crazy the way some people have treated their friends. I have seen some people try to lord things over, or think they're the leader, and also try to push their way on their friends. I have had friends who have actually thrown fits because something didn't turn out the way they wanted it to. I have lost friends because I wouldn't allow them to dictate to me. A friendship is meant to be enjoyed. Friends support each other. Nobody will ever see eye to eye on everything. Everyone has their own opinion. We need to know when to give and when to take, when to have a voice and when to let it go. Life is too short to hold something against someone, especially if it's something small. Once a friend and I bought matching shirts for the fun of it when I was a teen and a third friend became upset over it. This third friend became distant. Why do we become so narrow minded that we let small things come in-between us and our friends? Why can't we love and not hate? I love to create good memories with my friends. I want to learn and grow with them. I will continue to be open, nonjudgmental, and forgiving. Through this I have created friendships that can last a lifetime.

Getting ready to walk to my in-laws' house I recall how I was someone who liked to allow friends to choose an activity. I had fun trying new things and just being easy going. Being a wife and mother it's hard to get out. Ben is someone who will drop what he's doing if someone needs help. But, when someone invites us out to dinner or tries to include us in an activity we never go. It's not that we don't want to go but something always happens to keeps us from going. Some friends have been lost to this. A friendship often doesn't last when it feels one-sided. Ben and I can't expect our friends to always do what we want or come over to our place all the time and vice versa. We need to mix it up! Let our friends make some choices of their own. If they come over and try the things we like, then we need to try some things they like.

I've found that in marriage it's not easy keeping a friendship with friends who are single. I've found that there is a big difference between single life and married life. Even though we have a few single friends that feel like family, I've found it easier to be friends with those who are also in a relationship or married and have kids. I thought it was very hard for a spouse to feel included when friends were single! In my experience, it was very frustrating. Ben's friends used to be mostly single. This caused me to feel like the third wheel and I have seen the expressions on the single friend's face looking uncomfortable as the third wheel. I think the best thing to do in this case is one-on-one time, or make it a group of friends so no one feels left out. I would think that as adults we could get past these things, but emotions are emotions and often they seem to not make sense. I remember a time where all of Ben's friends were single. I was very uncomfortable. I started to wonder if Ben envied their singleness. It was hard for me to adjust to a world where I was supposed to belong but felt like I wasn't accepted. Through all my studying, I finally got it through my thick head that being accepted did not matter. What mattered was me being accepting and having a hospitable attitude. As I started to put this into practice it was not awkward to be around Ben's single friends anymore. It closed the gap between the single and married life.

I learned that I shouldn't focus on how friendly someone else is, but rather focus on my friendliness. If someone is having problems, then I need to seek that problem out and help that friend through it. I don't need to harden my heart and think that I need to retaliate because my friend has an attitude. The attitude may have nothing to do with me.

I have discovered when a friend or family member brings nothing but evil into the relationship that we need to let this friendship go. Matthew 5:29-30 says, "If your right eye causes you to sin, pluck it out and cast it from you; for it is more profitable for you that one of your members perish, than for your whole body to be cast into hell. And if your right hand causes you to sin, cut it off and cast it from you; for it is more profitable for you that one of your members perish, than for your whole body to be cast into hell." Matthew 18:15-17 says, "Moreover if your brother sins against you, go and tell him his fault between you and him alone. If he hears you, you have gained your brother. But if he will not hear, take with you one or two more, that 'by the mouth of two or three witnesses every word may be established.' And if he refuses to hear them, tell it to the church. But if he refuses even to hear the church, let him be to you like a heathen and a tax collector." When someone sins against us we first need to try to make it right. But if this person refuses and continues to bring hate and destruction into our lives it's better to cast this person from us so we may save ourselves. This is a hard and difficult thing to do, but will bring peace when the toxic person is let go. I have struggled in this area with Willy. He won't stop telling lies or spreading rumors.

Coming up to the house I see the kids on the lawn sitting in their camp chairs and Ben preparing for a Mother's Day barbeque. My father-in-law bellows from the porch, "Here comes the hippie." I just smile as he says more hurtful things. I think about those who have a great friendship with their in-laws and how they are truly blessed. But, in a lot of cases, like mine, the in-laws or parents seem to butt-in too much. My father-in-law has placed himself as the most important person. This has created hurt and frustration running through my side of the family. But, I realize that my father-in-law is reacting from past hurts. I love all of them and it's hard to see them struggle and be at odds. Ben and I are stuck in the middle. Regardless, we still need to show respect and be loving, even though I want to run around screaming and pull out my hair. But, we can lovingly, without being snappy, not allow them to over-step boundaries. Ben and I need to be in accordance with each other on how far is too far. We need to be honest with our parents if we can, although some things might be considered too much of a touchy subject. We may want to be careful how we word things with them. Then there are subjects where there isn't much we can do without starting a war. I have learned that it's best to just be patient. I need to help the situation be as peaceful as possible. If a war starts I'm not the only one who is affected. This will affect more than one family unit. Even though it starts with me and an in-law or parent it can spread to my spouse and over to the other side of the family. This can get way out of hand. So, I just need to bite the tongue and just love, be polite, and show consideration.

I know that if we didn't live on my in-laws' property it wouldn't be so hard. I would find myself calling them or getting online to communicate. I would also make time to go out to dinner or have barbeques, or maybe have one-on-one time with each of them. This could bring us closer. But since we are next-door neighbors on the same property I want to find a way to get away from them. I feel like I need a vacation from them. I have learned through all this that when we're around each other too much it causes issues. This is where the saying "with distance the heart grows fonder" comes into play. It is human nature for the parents to butt-in to their children's lives. This is never healthy for a marriage unless we ask for the butting-in. If Ben and I need butting in then we should find someone who is not close to the situation such as a pastor, an elder of a church, or a counselor. They should guide us in the right direction without any prejudice.

Anyone who tries to butt into our marriage without permission will create problems. We do our best to overcome them. There may come times when we have to say something to the person who's butting in. We need to keep in mind that we should confront this person in a loving manner without lashing out with anger and hate, whether it's a relative or friend.

Respect is not just about doing what you're told! This means to love, to defer to authority, to bless them with good deeds, to speak good of them, and honor them with our conduct of the person we've became. We do not have to agree with them all the time, or have to say yes to everything. But everything must be done in love. If we have to take a stand against them because they're being harmful to themselves or others, then we do it in love. Watching the confrontations that surround my in-laws, I can say that all but the youngest knows how to show respect. Willy has yelled with foul language, he has talked bad and threatened his parents, and he's played games to get his desired outcome. Ben and my younger sister-in-law show the most respect. They're not afraid to admit when they're in the wrong and seek to right the wrong. They don't talk down to their parents and are willing to stick around through the hardships. The two oldest children are not in the picture much but, when they are around, they show respect. I look to my father-in-law who is a Vietnam vet. He has earned his respect. The country should always show respect to soldiers. They put their lives in danger to fight for us, a country that seems to be falling apart.

Last Mother's Day, Willy walked into the house with two hanging baskets. He gives one to his mom and gave the other one to me. I was a little flustered. I said, "Thank you!" while wondering what he was up to. It was very nice of him to get me a gift. I'm not his mom. But I'm also leery of what it might represent. Was it his way of apologizing for the hurt he's caused, or was he trying to work us over to get us to a place to hurt us again? I was civil in my attitude toward him, but I haven't allowed him close. Not until I see that he's stopped saying lies about the family.

With brothers and or sisters we see a love-hate relationship between one another. It becomes more of a competition and a rivalry. This applies to sibling in-laws also. We know each other's darkest secrets, annoying habits, and best qualities. We can be each other's greatest enemies or closest friends. Sibling relationships can sometimes be the hardest to understand. We may not get along but are expected to because we are blood or in-laws. We just need to love and be there for each other, even though we might not get along all the time or agree with each other.

Even though I keep Willy at a distance, I watch his three kids for him and my in-laws. Ben has also been there for Willy whenever Willy needed a helping hand. We also need to have open communication and enjoy friendly competition and rivalry, knowing the boundaries and not trying to overstep them. There is deep history behind us. We should do our best not to let the evil of this life tear our sibling relationship apart. We should stay in touch with each other even though we are mad or upset with each other.

When we're wronged by a sibling it can become the hardest thing to forgive because we are so close and connected. It will hurt the worst. But, if we can overcome the hurt and forgive, we will have set the basis for all our relationships. Relationships with our siblings can teach us how to function with other friendships because we take our first steps with them. We need to seek forgiveness and start communicating with our siblings that we've disowned. Turning away from a sibling even if they are in-laws isn't easy either. I'm at a complete loss where Willy is concerned. I often wonder how I'm supposed to function around him. I don't hate him as a person but I do hate how he treats us, including how he treats his parents. Keeping my distance isn't easy either but sometimes it must be done. I do the only thing I know how to do, which is what the Bible has taught me: to remove my presence and treat him as a tax collector. I pray for him and hope. I can only imagine how hurt his parents are.

Then there are kids. Younger children can sometimes be difficult. As parents, we are to be their protectors, teachers, disciplinarians, and comforters. We need to apply a healthy balance in their early lives because the way they are raised will affect what they become as adults. I haven't been a perfect parent. I have failed so many times. I get frustrated and have yelled and screamed often just like my mom. But I apologize when I'm in the wrong, something else my mom did. I find that the older my kids get, the more argumentative they are and the less patience I struggle with.

Matthew 18: 2-9 says, "Then Jesus called a little child to him, set him in the midst of them, and said, 'Assuredly, I say to you, unless you are converted and become as little children, you will by no means enter the kingdom of heaven. Therefore whoever humbles himself as a little child is greatest in the kingdom of heaven. Whoever receives one little child like this in my name receives me. Whoever causes one of these little ones who believe in me to sin, it would be better for him if a millstone were hung around his neck, and he were drowned in the depth of the sea. Woe to the world because of offenses! For offenses must come, but woe to that man by whom the offence comes!'" This applies to all people—not just children.

I know this is about adults being as little children but I think on it for a minute. To completely trust and love as a child. Yes, I have offended! I have caused my children to sin through my reactions to them. My middle son and I are often at odds. There are times where I have promised him something but couldn't follow through due to circumstances. He would holler and scream, "I hate you! I wish I never had a mom!" This would hurt. He would continue to throw a fit until he got something he wanted. I began to see that this was creating a selfish, stubborn monster. So now, when this happens, I say, "Go ahead and hate me! I love you and I'm doing what's best for you." It no longer hurts when he screams those words because they are just words. I know he loves me. He was acting out this way because he knew I would cave in.

We need to be careful with how we raise our children. We all have right and wrong ways on how to raise a child. The way we raise our children is most likely the way that child will view God. If we become distant and are not there for that child, then that child may see God the same way. If we are there for the child and the child can always come to us with his or her needs, then the child will see God this way, which is the right way. I chose to love so my children will learn to love, to forgive so my children will forgive, to be patient so my children will be patient, to have joy so my children will have joy, to have goodness so my children will have goodness, to have gentleness so my children will be gentle, to have self-control so my children will have self-control, to have faith and hope so my children will have faith and hope. I have just taught my children the fruits of the spirit found in Galatians 5.

This also applies to sin. If I practice adultery, fornication, uncleanness, lewdness, idolatry, sorcery, hatred, contentions, jealousies, outbursts of wrath, selfish ambition, dissensions, heresies, envy, murders, drunkenness, revelries, and the like, my children will learn these too.

Raising children in the right way will be one of our greatest accomplishments. This doesn't always leave room for a friendship. Friendship probably won't come until they are adults themselves. But this is okay – I don't stress over it. Ben and I are to guide our children in making the right decisions until they become accountable for themselves. As parents, we need to have patience and make time for each of them. We need to know that they each are different individuals and they each need a different type of relationship from us. We need to show that they are loved the same even though it may be in different ways. Ben and I need to not discipline in anger or hate. We could go overboard and it can become abuse. We need to let the punishment fit the crime and make sure they understand why they are being punished. We don't want to confuse them. Children are precious. They are a gift regardless of how they come into the world, whether they were wanted or not, and we do not want to lose their trust. Once we lose their trust they will build walls against us. This can cause them resentment which will become bitterness. This will cause the child to have issues with his or her emotions, relationships, and actions when he or she is older.

I'm enjoying my kids while they are little. I hug them often and spend as much time as I can with them. This time with them flies by fast. Soon they'll be in their pre-teens, like my oldest, and hitting puberty. This isn't a fun time. They'll start to have minds of their own and be argumentative. This has stretched my will for trying to have true love in reacting to my oldest kid's outbursts. I find, for myself, I have to walk away at times to regroup and think things out before it gets too heated. Pre-teens at this age, I am finding out, find it hard to think they are wrong about anything. I can't say what comes after this since I have not experienced it yet, but I hope it gets better.

Love, marriage, friendships, siblings, and children are an everyday part to our lives. Love should be an everyday occurrence in all our relationships. I will keep my heart open and the love flowing.

17. HAPPILY LOVING AFTER

"For it is the God who commanded light to shine out of darkness, who has shone in our hearts to give the light of the knowledge of the glory of God in the face of Jesus Christ."
~2 Corinthians 4:6

    I smiled at my father-in-law today. I find myself smiling at him more often, even when he is trying to be hurtful. I find that his opinion of me no-longer has power to bring me down. We have more good moments than we did in the past. Choosing to love him brought a lot of change. When we choose to love others by action and through affection we are the face of Jesus. We inspire and encourage in truth. We are living out our own individual ministry. Our loving actions minister to those around us. We give hope. But, when we say we are believers and act out in hate we are great deceivers. We will bring death instead of life. Our ministry becomes false. We become snakes spreading venom that will miss guide and destroy. I fell into this hate. But when I hit bottom my eyes were open. I saw beyond my emotions. I saw how my life led up to the point of destruction. I also saw how this destruction brought me to a turning point.
    When I started dating Ben, it was all about being thrilled and overjoyed in finding a relationship, experiencing the tingling sensations, and the breathlessness of excitement when in each other's company. I no longer felt that void that was felt before. I believed that it was because I met Mr. Right that I was finally complete. But, soon after we married, life happened. My world fell apart drastically. I was lost once again, more so than I was before I married. I expected certain things and became disappointed. My in-laws took over our marriage and kids which caused hardships. My husband became distant. My past also caused issues. I began to hate. I hated the

circumstances and people around me, and I hated myself. I was too focused on what was going on around me that I totally missed what was going on within me. I so hated everything that was going on around me after my marriage that I allowed the negative feelings to take over, but when the time came, that moment I chose to love, when I chose to work on myself, I put each piece of my puzzle back together. I found my completeness. It was like when you buy a used puzzle, you have to put it together to see if all the pieces are there. Putting myself back together I found all my pieces. I found strength, power, hope, peace, self-confidence, my calling, and, most important, I discovered true love.

18. DIFFERENT TYPES OF LOVE

"And now abide faith, hope, love, these three; but the greatest of these is love."
~1 Corinthians 13:13

The church I went to as a kid loved to talk about love and the different meanings, although I never truly understood it until I lived it. Agape is the type of love that comes from within, it is the love of all loves. With this love, I can forgive, I can fight for what's right, I can sacrifice myself and serve others. Agape love covers all. This is the most pure and truest form of love. I like to think that this type of love is the whole version of love, that the other types are broken pieces from this version. Like a vase that has been broken, all the pieces are fragments of the whole vase. Put it all back together and what do I have? A whole.

This is the type of love Jesus has for us, to sacrifice himself for our sins. He took all his glory and became human to understand us better, to get to know our struggles and weaknesses, and to guide us. He did all this knowing that he will be giving his life for us. I believe, whether others believe or not, that Jesus is the best example to follow in the area of love. I now have better understanding. I can love people even if I'm hated. I can sacrifice my time and energy on those who want to cause me harm. Jesus did. He was hated by many and accused, with many wanting to bring Him harm, yet He gave his life for all.

My love for Ben started out with Eros. This version is a love of romance, with all the zings and electricity. This is what most likely will bring two people together in a relationship. We all love these feelings. But, sadly, these feelings don't last. It's not good to base a relationship off of this type of love. I have seen many people do this. It's good and healthy to have it in our relationship or marriage, though, if we can keep it from fading. With every positive, there is a negative, even in love. This type of love can also be very dangerous if only one person is feeling this type of love. These types of people can be stocker-ish, jealous enough to cause harm, even depressed to the point of harming themselves. This is not good.

As Ben and my relationship grew, after we lost the Eros version of love in our struggles, we found Phileo. This type of love is found in families and among friends. This is a brotherly type of love, a love between best friends. We can trust each other and have faith in each other. When we love people with this love, we will find that we will go to them when we're having problems and need help, and we can tell them our secrets. With this love, we will go the extra mile for our friends or family. We will seek their advice on things, whether they are important or not. This love is a love that we give to anyone that we feel close to. With the closeness of this love Ben and I were able to restore the Eros version of love. It connected us like a puzzle.

As I grew in love, and my relationship with Ben grew, we found Storge love for each other. Storge is a love of mutual respect, of acceptance, and of a feeling of safety. This is a love that we can mostly find in families. This love can give us the feeling of security. This love my not be exciting but at least we know we belong. I've heard that this love can be boring but I don't agree. Sure, we may not have the zings and electricity, but who needs that all the time and with every relationship. It feels good to be able to feel secure that we belong somewhere, to feel accepted for who we are, and to feel respected by the people we respect. This love has brought Ben and I very close. One thing I wanted most is mutual respect, acceptance, and the feeling of safety. I have found security in Ben's arms. We went through hardships built by our negative emotions that have refined us to who we are for each other today. This wasn't easy to go through but we kept making choices that brought us up the staircase of love one step after the other. We now have Agape love for each other.

As I have looked back I have wanted to warn people to be careful where emotions and feelings of love can lead. It's so easy to overstep with the emotions of love, allowing them to become emotions of hate. Any relationship will start out good and pure, but when we invest more of ourselves, other emotions will come into our relationships. One big emotion is jealousy, and then you have covetousness and lust. Jealousy or covetousness is never a good thing. Lust will lead astray, and so it should be dealt with and defeated. It is not an emotion of love. Strong desire, on the other hand, if channeled right doesn't have to be bad. You can have strong desire for your spouse, want to spend time with him or her, want to do nice things for him or her, and have a strong desire to love and protect. This is the only time that this is alright. If these feeling are for another, when bound in a marriage, it will destroy that marriage. If experiencing this in something or someone other than a spouse, then it needs to stop. If experiencing this when not married, then it still needs to stop. We need to be careful because strong desire can create the feeling of jealousy and this also applies to lust.

Emotions are a very complicated thing. We all need to make sure our hearts are in the right place when dealing with our emotions. We need to ask ourselves why we're feeling what we are and if it's truly a right emotion to feel. Also, if it's an act that's made us upset we need to ask ourselves if it's a reason to get so upset about. For example, when someone's actions cause our emotions to get stirred up and out of whack we need to rethink those actions through and check ourselves to see if our emotions are overreacting. I don't want to let my emotions rule me. I need to rule my emotions. I now know what love is, I know when I overstep, and I understand my emotions and keep them in check. Negative emotions can lead to being controlling and hateful. I never want to go through those emotions again. Discovering true love hasn't been easy. But, if I had it to do all over again, I would. The wisdom I have gained, and the love I have found, has become great rewards.

19. FIGHTING THE GOOD FIGHT

"The moon and stars shine bright at night,
Strength becomes stronger after each battle,
and love is brightest and strongest in the midst of darkness."
~Quote from H.E. Olsen

    I still have hardships and difficulties. I struggle with what to say and what to do in some situations. But I don't struggle to love. Loving didn't happen overnight. It was a growing process. I had to forgive and let go over and over. There was so much negativity around me that it was easy to get caught up in it again, but not as deep as I was before. Loving my father-in-law was not easy at first. It took a lot of work. But I chose to move forward in my positivity. I smiled when I didn't want to and it became easier over time. When he was in a bad mood I learned to listen to the soul rather than his words. I could see that my father-in-law's hurt and pain were very deep. Soon I was able to tell him, "I love you." This became easier over time too. I no longer saw him as a bully but as someone with deep negative emotions. After a while we had a relationship, although a difficult one. My father-in-law is now failing in health. His body is becoming weaker and weaker fighting heart disease. He now struggles to walk with a cane. In his fear and depression, he has gone back to not truly accepting me again. I have come full circle. But I understand better, unlike the time I left my Granny. I will stay and be here for him and the family, wanted or not.

    I will always be grateful to my father-in-law for bringing the best out in me through our relational difficulties—for helping me become the person I am today. Without having been bullied by him, I wouldn't have become the strong, loving individual that I am today. He was an answer to my prayer of wanting to learn to love God's way. I rejoice in the difficulties that brought me to this understanding.

I now have the understanding that I was the one who put myself in that colorless box that became my dark world. Letting hate fester in me did this. It's so easy to fall into negativity, but it takes hard work and determination to grow in love. With each step in the process of learning to love comes freedom to the soul. A healing where hurt and hate created wounds. Forgiveness is a tool of love that brings the wounds to healing. I walked through a lot of forgiveness. I am no longer blinded by the gray fog of hate that almost destroyed me. I began to see that the world is not black and white and filled with gray shadows, but colorful, with amazing bright and dark colors. Once I chose to love, its light shined into my box, through the fog, shattering the negative world I created and bringing life, beautiful and colorful life.

I have learned that hard places and struggles are stepping stones to help me grow. I can create light, through my faith, in myself, from a dark world. The negativity and hardships of this world become a staircase to walk up helping me grow and become stronger. The deeper and darker the struggle, the brighter my light will shine. No longer do I shy away or run from hardships, I look forward to them. I want to learn, grow, and become stronger. No matter how deep and dark the enemy wants to take me, they will see that in the deepest darkest parts I will shine the brightest, because I shine with the love of God.

The light of love can be a resting place for those struggling in the dark. Love each bully - they are hurting from deep pain. Love the haters - this gives them no fuel for the fire. Love is letting go. We live in a world of chaos and uncontrolled choices, where people are living by emotions alone. Not seeing the harm they are creating or the damage done, with each being selfish and hateful in their box worlds, bringing greater darkness to our world. But, even in this, I will fight the good fight and love.

1 Corinthians 13

Though I speak with the tongues of men and of angels,
But have not love,
I have become sounding brass or a clanging symbol.
And though I have the gift of prophecy,
And understand all mysteries,
And though I have all faith,
So I can remove mountains,
But have not love,
I am nothing.
And though I bestow all my goods to feed the poor,
And though I give my body to be burned,
But have not love,
It profits me nothing.
Love suffers long and is kind;
Love does not envy;
Love does not parade itself,
Is not puffed up;
Does not behave rudely,
Does not seek its own,
Is not provoked,
Thinks no evil;
Does not rejoice in iniquity,
But rejoices in the truth;
Bears all things,
Believes all things,
Hopes all things,
Endures all things.
Love never fails.

But whether there are prophecies, they will fail; whether there are tongues, they will cease; whether there is knowledge, it will vanish away. For we know in part and prophecy in part. But when that which is perfect has come, then that which is in part will be done away. When I was a child, I spoke as a child, I understood as a child, I thought as a child; but when I became a man, I put away childish things. For now we see in a mirror, dimly, but then face to face. Now I know in part, but then I shall know just as I also am known.

And now abide
Faith,
Hope,
Love,
These three;
But the greatest of these is love.

ABOUT THE AUTHOR

H.E. Olsen has been through deep trials that brought her to discover the true meaning of love. Confronted with pain and suffering, she studied mental illness and behavioral dysfunctions to better understand herself and be of help to others. Through it all, a desire has been born in H.E. Olsen to tell her story to inspire others, and share her new-found understanding of love. She is married with three amazing kids.

H.E. Olsen may be reached through the following platforms:
www.holsen68.wordpress.com
www.facebook.com/author.h.e.olsen
www.twitter.com/holsen68

EDITOR'S NOTE

This book qualifies for the publisher's *One-for-One Challenge*. *Buy a copy, and publisher will donate $1 dollar to establish resource centers for orphanages in developing countries*, where these amazing kids may learn to read, dream, and grow. Just because they are orphans doesn't mean their future has to be limited. Learn more at www.kharispublishing.com.

As a social enterprise, Kharis Publishing is committed to give voice to under-represented authors by publishing their books free of charge; and also empower orphans through literacy initiatives. Join our online community at www.kharispublishing.com.